1803 – 1876

Orestes Brownson

Orestes Augustus Brownson, 1803-1876

Orestes Brownson

Sign of Contradiction

10/8/99

To Vincent
& Suzanne, Fondly,
Bob

R. A. Herrera

 ISI

ISI BOOKS
Intercollegiate Studies Institute
WILMINGTON, DELAWARE

Cataloging-in-Publication Data

Herrera, Robert A.
    Orestes A. Brownson : sign of
    contradiction / by R. A. Herrera. --
    Wilmington, DE : ISI Books, 1999.

        p.   cm.

    Includes bibliographical references.
    ISBN 1-882926-33-1
       1. Brownson, Orestes Augustus, 1803–1876.
    I. Title

B908.B64 H47 1999   99-71453
191--dc21   CIP

Published in the United States by

ISI Books
P.O. Box 4431
Wilmington, DE 19807-0431
www.isi.org

Design and layout by HeartLand Publications, LLC

Printed on acid-free paper.
Manufactured in the United States of America

10 9 8 7 6 5 4 3 2 1

To the memory of two good and wise men,
my father, S. J. Herrera, who introduced me to the
thought of Orestes Brownson, and
Doctor Russell Kirk, who, by his sagacious
guidance, made me realize its importance.

Contents

Acknowledgments

I wish to express my gratitude to Mr. Ed Garea for his invaluable help in preparing and editing the typescript, to the Firestone Library of Princeton University, to the McLaughlin Library of Seton Hall, and to Miss Brooke Daley and her gifted staff at ISI.

Prologue

Orestes Augustus Brownson was a puzzle to his contemporaries. Considered something of a prophet, he was actually more a ponderous gadfly. He was anything but routine, and considered by many to be a great man. Though he often spoke of himself as a plain, untutored woodsman, Brownson was the ultimate auto-didact and became a monument of vast, albeit patchy, erudition. Of the original members of the Transcendentalist Club, he was the most philosophically inclined. He was also the most rigorous thinker and by far the most aggressive personality. When he converted to Roman Catholicism, the popular voice spoke of red hats and soaring ambition. He never again occupied center stage, except for a brief period during the Civil War as a vigorous Union apologist. It was his journalistic labors as editor (*Boston Quarterly Review*, *Brownson's Quarterly Review*) and his status as American Catholic oracle that kept his name alive and his thought in circulation to a large audience of a given intellectual and religious cast.

In the century and a quarter since his death in 1874, Brownson's fame has ebbed to the point of disappearance, his name almost forgotten except by members of Catholic debating societies. When vandals toppled his memorial bust from

its pedestal at New York City's Sherman Park in 1937, it took
a lengthy hiatus before being identified as Brownson. It was
then placed on the campus of Fordham University, uncom-
fortably close to the statue of his *bête noire*, Archbishop
Hughes. Brownson has been reduced to the status of a color-
ful eccentric, a peripheral crank, a simple nuisance. From a
puzzle he has become a curiosity. Russell Kirk noted that
"something like a conspiracy of silence has kept his name out
of the histories of American thought"[1]—sad and inexplicable
fate for a man called America's Newman by Père Gratry, and
compared by others to Doctor Johnson and even to St.
Augustine. Brownson's hyperkineticism, his egotism, and
bizarre personality made him an enigmatic figure, difficult to
comprehend and to like. The words of his friend, Isaac
Hecker, "wherever he was he was felt," were to the point.[2]
The man whom Bishop Roosevelt Bayley called *Ursus Major*
could scarcely go unnoticed.

His conversion to Roman Catholicism— "Catholicity" as
he preferred to call it—was both a paradox and a puzzle to
his contemporaries. He abandoned his former associates, the
privileged New England milieu into which he had been
admitted, to enter a church that was both alien and unsavory.
His disregard for the public orthodoxy, both before and subsequent to his conversion, was unsettling to the American
public which, as was pointed out by de Tocqueville and
Charles Dickens, does not applaud those who fail to treat
their favorite icons with due reverence. He also succeeded in
mobilizing the resentment of his former colleagues, many of
whom interpreted his conversion as further proof of his mental instability. How could a man of his undoubted gifts pass
into Roman Catholicism, seen by New Englanders as the
atavistic religion of the Irish underclass?

He was not welcomed unreservedly into the Catholic fold, which proceeded to entangle him in unfortunate intramural conflicts. The attempt was made to change his philosophical method and style and subordinate his eclectic genius to the forms of an otiose scholasticism. He became immersed in the twists and turns, evasions and subterfuges, of clerical politics. He became a target for several Catholic factions, some of which he had attempted to defend. Yet he did not regret his conversion. His salvation was at stake and the devil takes the hindmost.

Orestes Brownson began his career as a radical liberal and ended it ostensibly as a hidebound conservative, moving from utopian socialism to ultramontane Catholicism. However, in spite of shifts and reevaluations, neither ever succeeded in eliminating the other. The encyclopedic nature of his work often led to dissonances and contradictions in his writings. The celerity with which he changed his views was, in his opinion, the fruit of experience and profound consideration, and he took umbrage at being called a "weathercock." In later life Brownson exhibited a greater uniformity of thought and principle. Even during his liberal hiatus of 1860-1864 there is no radical change, but rather a continuing struggle between the resuscitated ideals of his youth and later conservative accretions. The end of the struggle, and this perhaps only on the public level, came with the promulgation of Pope Pius IX's encyclical, *Quanta Cura* in 1864, with the *Syllabus of Errors*.

A curious mixture of Roundhead and Cavalier, a rugged Yankee attracted by Southern gentility, Brownson was a puzzle to the effete members of the Transcendentalist Club. He was self-taught, having had practically no formal education— the autodidact of autodidacts in an age of them. His voluminous reading and draconian study habits produced an abundant harvest. Immediately after his conversion, Brownson immersed himself in Catholic thought and modes of exposition, writing in the scholastic mode and citing Petavius, Cano, Vazquez, and other worthies. Though Brownson would later admit that such an abrupt change of pace was unfortunate, he carried it through admirably.

His philosophical enthusiasms and extensive correspondence made him familiar with contemporary European thought to an extent unmatched in his milieu. Like most Americans born under the sign of the 1789 French Revolution, Brownson was enamored of progress, the new, radical solutions, fads, and utopian social schemes. Although many of his enthusiasms were short-lived, while they lasted he was their fearsome champion. He cultivated bluster as an artform, the protective covering of a timid man, who, when he began to preach, would emerge drenched in perspiration.

A hirsute Vermonter who could be engagingly civil or abrasively uncouth, Brownson was proud of his English heritage. He believed that it formed the essential core of the nation, though he repeatedly condemned English and American materialism and commercial hubris. When American Nativists persecuted Irish immigrants, he rose to their defense, albeit in a manner irritating to both. This brought him under attack from both Know-Nothing groups and prominent Irish-American prelates. While demanding that the Nativists cease their persecution, he found it a difficult task to be both Catholic and American. In spite of his longstanding belief (modified near the end of his life) that America and Catholicism were a providential conjunction that would ensure a glorious future, he was often the object of ill-humored, often malicious, attacks from prelates and the Catholic press. As he once stated, his tenure within Catholicism was more like a bed of spikes than a bed of roses.[3]

Brownson was not diplomatic. He spoke his mind directly and loudly. As Archbishop Hughes advised Rome, Brownson relished controversy. He succeeded in alienating the Irish, the English Tractarians, and the Jesuits, among others. In his later years he exchanged negative opinions on Catholics with Montalembert, ascribing the vice of dishonesty to them, noting a cavalier attitude toward truth as characteristic of prelates.

Brownson loathed Abolitionists in spite of his negative view of slavery. He believed them to be radicals on the move, with slavery only a convenient point of departure. Like Lincoln, he had a low opinion of the Negro race, perceiving them as inferior to Caucasians, degraded and vicious. He came to advocate legal equality and Negro suffrage with reluctance only because of the vicissitudes of the Civil War. Moreover, again like Lincoln (of whom he had a poor opinion), Brownson favored colonization, though he dismissed this idea outright once Negroes were mobilized by the Union army. He continued to fear that the liberated slaves, if not subjected to some form of apprenticeship, would sow the seeds of future national unsettlement, possibly taking the form of an Africanization of the South.

Many noteworthy personalities of the age suffered at his hands. Catholics were not exempted. He attacked John Henry Newman and his *Essay on the Development of Doctrine*, which perplexed and irked him. American prelates egged him on. He disapproved of the members of the Tractarian Movement, dismissing them as priggish dons attracted to Catholicity by aesthetic and intellectual, not religious, motives. Newman reacted negatively to Brownson's criticism, but recommended him for an appointment at the recently founded Catholic University at Dublin where he served as rector. Sir John (later Lord) Acton endorsed Newman's initiative, considering Brownson the most penetrating American thinker of the day. The project was frustrated, as was Newman's bishopric *in partibus*, because of clerical opposition. While Newman was later more kindly treated (and then censured again) by Brownson, several prominent American prelates became the objects of his wrath. In the front ranks of these was Archbishop Hughes of New York.

Brownson's early life was a search for both a father and a foundational authority. He found them in God and the Catholic Church. He began and ended as an enthusiast and dogmatist, though situated at different points of the spectrum. He began as a fervent Utopian, sympathizing with the feminism of the Saint-Simonians. Later he became aware of the negative aspect of its ideology, and ended his life as something of a patriarchal curmudgeon. An early enthusiasm for the thought of Cousin was replaced by that of Leroux, which remained an important influence despite a later attraction to Gioberti. As a professedly Catholic thinker, Brownson followed an Augustinian orientation while disengaging himself from party Thomism. The insistence of some Catholics on the primacy of St. Thomas Aquinas struck him as similar to the Protestant attitude toward the Bible.

Brownson was highly intellectualized, very much self-absorbed, delighting in unpacking the ultimate logical conclusions of any premise. Yet, at least initially, he oscillated from one set of conclusions to another. He admitted that he could not be certain whether his convictions would be tomorrow what they were today.[4] Whether these variations corresponded to a progressive deepening of his thought (as he believed), or to other causes, among which his penchant for change must be included, remains a matter for conjecture. Perhaps his profession as journalist, which heightened his sensitivity to the fluctuations of public opinion, played a role.

Brownson often accused the press of lowering the tone of public discourse.

He began by equating Christianity with democracy, adumbrating a kind of liberation theology that employed Christianity to further democracy's progress toward an earthly paradise. Though his sympathy for the poor and downtrodden perdured, Brownson came to distrust the masses and to consider radical democracy as a threat to civilization. His increasingly elevated view of the spiritual realm and its concrete realization in the Catholic Church reduced the social and political domains from the status of ends to those of means, a complete reversal. He came to dismiss his early convictions as mere humbug!

Brownson's intellectual and practical life became centered on religion. Though pious, he was hardly attuned to the higher reaches of spirituality, contemptuous of "mysticism" as self-serving sentimentality bonded to undisciplined flights of imagination. He was not given to corporeal penance. Although he made attempts to meditate according to St. Ignatius Loyola's method (given in his *Ejercicios Espirituales*), he did not succeed, and an article on the Ignatian method shows little familiarity with it.[5] Brownson was hardly an ascetic, though reports of his gargantuan appetite and consumption of vast amounts of beef and whiskey were probably exaggerated. The same cannot be said of his monumental bouts of gout. He often suggested that conversion to Catholicism had weaned him away from puritanical habits of mind and contributed to his increasing girth. Nevertheless, other residues of Yankee puritanism would dog his steps with amazing persistence.

Vigor, profusion, logical élan, and short-term consistency characterized his intellectual posture. Brownson wrote in the third person, emphasizing his role as authoritative teacher. He did not dance. The light and holy escaped him. A meat and potatoes thinker, occasionally a happy phrase or insight interrupts the rigorous argument and constant hammering home of a point. His best pieces are produced by means of a logical battering that reenacts the lengthy chess games he played with son Orestes, Jr. Nevertheless, it must be admitted that, more often than not, Brownson makes a good case for the thesis he advances. He is a physical thinker, at his best when grappling with a problem, charging mace in hand to crush the enemy.

There is a more human side to Orestes Brownson: emotional, even tender, hidden under his aggressive fanfaronade. This side was directed toward his love for wife and children, Catholicity, America, and, strange to say, the world of nature, particularly that of his native Vermont. He was the autocrat of the breakfast table and was accused of aspiring to be the autocrat of the intellectual world. It must have been torture for most of his family, excepting perhaps Henry, to discuss Kant's *a priori* forms of intuition at the breakfast table. His often impetuous generosity and strong attachment to friends suggest that Brownson was not a logical automaton. He often declared that he was primarily an emotional creature, and so he was. Many of his writings and lectures were simply convenient vehicles of emotional discharge. His vaunted logical powers contained much of the instinctual.

Brownson never reached the heights to which he aspired, either on the national scene or on the personal, where his goal was to become a glorified version of John C. Calhoun. He was flawed in many ways, suffering from a vein of pettiness and resentment that can only be described as academic, though his correspondence shows that he attempted to curb its most irritating manifestations. Brownson was a professional in the best sense, a fine writer and editor graced with a bold and manly style—his favorite accolades. Ponderous, often lengthy to the point of weariness, he is addicted to verbal avalanches due, perhaps, to a conjunction of temperament and the financial exigencies of his profession.

He possessed the energy, persistence, and expertise necessary to become the major (at times sole) contributor to the journals he edited, and the intelligence to write many excellent journalistic pieces, and account for the near classic status of *The American Republic*. However, much of his work was mediocre; he routinely entered areas that were best left untouched and often applied criteria that were not germane to the subject at hand. To evaluate these flaws one must also consider the wide scope of his interests. Brownson wrote on nearly everything that occupied the attention and inflamed the imagination of his epoch, often with astonishing clarity and expertise.

His enthusiasm regarding the role of religion in social reform did not wane even when he passed on to a position in which Catholicity occupied the center. He advocated infusing the Christian spirit throughout a world that, if left to natural gravity, would regress to gentilism, *i.e.*, the primacy of the material order over the spiritual. Brownson's view of the depredations caused by original sin—Augustinian in inspiration—became more somber with advancing age. He moved away from the position advocated by Father Hecker, which he came to reject as semi-Pelagian, and toward the pessimism of a Donoso Cortés. Only grace is able to resist the gravity of weakened human nature. This belief came to chill his American optimism, with its infatuation with progress and change, although it would surface in episodes of varying durations.

Brownson was an enthusiastic believer in the American dream. The United States was a providential nation, a city on the hill, which would ultimately embrace Catholicity and become a beacon to the world. Much of this vision perdured even after he had become disenchanted with popular democracy and had repeatedly castigated the faults and vagaries of the American people. He was convinced that the American virtues of independence, sobriety, discipline, and courage would tilt them toward Catholicity in its ultramontane form. Brownson inspired this belief in Isaac Hecker, who incorporated it into the bloodstream of his religious congregation, the Society of St. Paul (Paulists). However, toward the end of his life, he came to believe that America and Americans were not only resistant to Catholicism but frankly opposed to it.

In many ways, Brownson was ahead of his time and prepared the way for the vicissitudes and conflicts of the twentieth (and perhaps the twenty-first) century. His influence extends to the theological, philosophical, and political. The liberal Brownson leads to the conciliar church, ecumenism, religious freedom, the separation of church and state, and social reform. The conservative Brownson was persuaded that alien ideologies had established themselves within the Church and were attempting to establish a counter-Christianity, a view that would lead to a reassessment of Vatican II. He was agonizingly aware of the depredations that a Catholicism become worldly and humanitarian would cause. He repeatedly marked the danger rampaging democracy presented to both the American republic and the Catholic Church. Though it is possible to choose either the liberal or the conservative Brownson as guide, a question remains: Was Brownson a prophet, a man who transcended his epoch, or simply an atavistic or utopian malcontent?

Orestes Augustus Brownson is the Catholic thinker *par excellence* of the United States. There are no rivals. The decks have been cleared. No Catholic thinker has equaled him in national prominence, international presence, density of thought, variety of concerns, or sheer volume. He was accepted by the Transcendentalists and corresponded with the European luminaries of the day: Cousin, Leroux, Newman, and Lord Acton among them. He was proposed for a teaching post at Harvard by Cousin and appointed to the newly founded Catholic University in Dublin by Newman. His *Boston Quarterly* and *Brownson's Quarterly* are considered landmarks in the history of American journalism. He was a thorn in the side of many but scarcely a common thorn, and his influence on the educated public and Catholic hierarchy was profound, if episodic. His thought was vigorous and has often been revisited and exploited.

Today Roman Catholicism and the United States, both zealously championed by Orestes Brownson, are heading toward the ultimate stage of popular democracy. The American republic has undergone a transmutation into a rainbow of fragmented groups, where no real unity of purpose or spirit can be clearly discerned. Immigration is drawing new masses to American shores rejecting any imperative to assimilate. The crucible cannot meld diverse elements lacking a common past, a shared vision, and a thought-out ideology. Catholicism has joined the Protestant churches, succumbing to the lure of gentilism in spite of pious protestations and galloping renewal.

Even when Brownson is not at his best, he is still worth reading. In these days of confusion, in which some believe the end-times are approaching, and others the terrestrial paradise, his works are not without relevance. Brownson was a major figure during a critical period of American and European history that witnessed the high-water mark of modernity. The Civil War, the year of Revolutions (1848), and the pontificate of Pius IX were events that characterized the epoch, one marked by other noteworthy events. The forces that would mold the future were already in the process of formation.

We encounter in Brownson's work many of today's most urgent problems: church and state, race, national unity, immigration, assimilation, sovereignty, the Constitution, and feminism. And then there are those vague and vast metaphysical questions that Brownson favored: the perennial questions concerning God, reality, human destiny, sin, and free will. There are few areas of human concern that his all-too-curious mind did not broach. A look back at Orestes Augustus Brownson, his world and works, is far more than a scholar's delight or an exercise in nostalgia. As an exercise in cultural genetics, it provides the reader with a novel optic with which to view and interpret the present.

I

Beginnings

In *The Convert*, Brownson remarks that "the historian of the aberrations of human nature during the last half century will... find this volume not unworthy of his attention."[1] Whether in order to delineate these aberrations, or to provide a more thorough account of them, Brownson wrote two additional works in which the biographical predominates: *Charles Elwood* and *The Spirit Rapper*. Whether he was consciously attempting to emulate Augustine or Rousseau, or simply following the contemporary penchant for self-justification of which John Henry Newman's *Apologia* would be the paradigm, this overabundance is characteristic of Brownson. He enjoyed studying himself and creating his own persona in the viewing, an animated *curriculum vitae* subject to ongoing correction.

Orestes Augustus Brownson was born in Stockbridge, Vermont, on September 15, 1803, one of five children, three boys and two girls. Sylvester Brownson, his father, was a native of Hartford County, Connecticut. His mother, Relief Metcalf, came from Keene, New Hampshire. The Brownsons were partisans of the Ethan Allen faction in the early border wars between the Yorkers and the Green Mountain boys.[2] At the age of six, Orestes, along with his twin sister Daphne, was placed with an old couple in the town of Royalton, Vermont. They are reported to have been honest and upright, very set in their ways, and of no particular religion. Life for Orestes and Daphne must have been drab, lacking the fascination and play of childhood. Years later, Brownson recalled: "properly speaking, I had no childhood, and have more of the child in my feelings now than at eight or ten years of age."[3] One pictures them as pathetic little stage adults, speaking in words and accents unsuited to their age.

Perhaps because of these narrow horizons, Orestes spent much of his time reading and daydreaming. The account of the passion of Jesus in the King James translation affected him greatly. It is not surprising that his childhood fantasies centered on religion. Brownson informs us that, at the early age of nine, he took part in a "theological dispute," in which he defended free will against the position of Jonathan Edwards. Solitude allowed his imaginative life to flourish. He mentions "long familiar conversations with the Lord" and "spiritual intercourse" with the Blessed Virgin Mary. Was this mere bragging, evidence of psychopathology, or an incipient touch of spirituality? Another interesting fact is that his progress in writing did not parallel that in reading, if we can believe Sir John (later Lord) Acton. Writing to Dollinger, Acton stated Brownson once confided to him that, in his eighteenth year, he did not know how to write.[4]

When the twins were fourteen, Relief moved her family to Ballston Spa, New York, not far from Vermont. There, Orestes received the only formal schooling of his life. Its content and duration remain nebulous; the more we know, the less impressive it is.[5] At Ballston Spa he worked as an apprentice and then as a journeyman in a printer's office; this became the point of departure for his later career. His religious stirrings continued, accompanied by serious doubts that dulled his former fervor. When Brownson was nineteen, he was very much affected at a Presbyterian Meeting House, and in October 1822, became a member of the Presbyterian Church at Ballston.[6] The unfavorable impression produced by this early experience caused Brownson to reserve his most scathing criticism for Presbyterianism. It was doubtless colored by the vicissitudes of later life.

He found the Presbyterian Church lacking in authority, composed of members who combine "a singular mixture of bigotry, uncharitableness, apparent zeal for God's glory, and a shrewd regard to the interests of this world."[7] At this time, Henry Brownson notes, his father was oppressed by an overpowering sense of the ubiquity of sin and a terrifying sense of alienation. The son naively remarks "evidently he was losing his wits."[8] Brownson survived this crisis. In 1823 he began to teach school at Stillwater, a village near Ballston Spa, and the following year accepted a teaching post in Detroit. There he fell seriously ill, reportedly with malaria, and spent most of the year 1825 convalescing, devoting himself to reading the Bible and Universalist publications.[9] A career in the ministry began to become progressively more attractive. In June of 1826, Orestes A. Brownson was ordained a Universalist preacher at Jaffrey, New Hampshire, passing "from so-called Orthodox Christianity to what is sometimes denominated liberal Christianity."[10] The following year, on June 19, 1827, he married Sally Healy at Elbridge, New York. She was a cousin of John Healy, Daniel Webster's law partner, and would prove to be an admirable and unusually compliant wife.

Brownson's decision to embrace Universalism, a diluted form of Congregationalism (itself a liberal protest against Calvinism), was influenced by a remarkable aunt who had heard Dr. Elhanan Winchester preach and was favorably impressed. He perused Winchester's works accompanied by his aunt's "brilliant" and "enthusiastic" commentaries. A further influence was Hosea Ballou who had fiercely attacked the entire fabric of orthodox Christianity. Though Brownson later attacked Ballou's treatise *On the Atonement* as the book most full of heresies ever published by the American press, at the time he admired Ballou's style, force, and uncompromising doctrine that "the salvation of all men is demanded as a right and not as a favor."[11] He took Ballou seriously, and being perversely logical, abandoned the Bible as authoritative, denied revelation, and rejected the divinity of Christ and future judgment. He was perfectly aware that Universalism could not be defended as a scriptural doctrine. By some strange occult compensation, Brownson was later to preach to Ballou's congregation at Boston; the largest he had yet addressed. He later observed that Universalism had made him not only non-Christian but anti-Christian.[12]

Brownson's career as a journalist began in 1828 when, at the age of twenty-five, he became the editor of the *Gospel Advocate*. He published in its pages a romantic creed, followed by an addendum in October of 1829. It is sincere, humanitarian, and vacuous. Perhaps imitating the five points of Calvinism as defined by the synod of Dort, it also consisted of five points. In this creed he declares his independence from anything mystical or supernatural and suggests the direction in which he contemplated moving. The object of Jesus, he declares, was to lead men to reform the world; "that all will finally become holy seems highly probable."[13] The publisher of the *Gospel Advocate*, U. F. Doubleday, commented unfavorably on Brownson's course toward atheism, and discharged him.[14] This was only a minor setback. His literary career not only continued, but also expanded to include political issues. He backed William H. Seward and the anti-

Masonic Party, opposing the evangelical sects who had agitated to discontinue Sunday mail delivery.

It was also about this time that Brownson began his career as a lecturer to supplement the family income. Over the next four decades he would travel as far as New Orleans and Mobile in the South, St. Louis in the West, and Montreal and Quebec in the North. In his lectures Brownson appealed primarily to the mind, not to the emotions. This was noted by Father Hecker, who recalled that while Brownson's physical appearance was impressive, he displayed a marked inability to stir the emotions. At this time he was about 6'2" in height, slim, and active. His black hair was brushed straight back from his forehead, and his deep-set eyes of mixed gray and hazel seemed to turn black when he got excited. Later, at Brook Farm, Georgiana Bruce called him "the unpolished, vehement, and positive man."[15] Before his conversion to Catholicism his regime was Spartan: a sparing diet, abstinence from spirits. Afterwards these habits were to change noticeably.

In October 1829, Brownson attended a lecture by Fanny Wright at Utica. He was enormously impressed by both the woman and her ideology. Throughout his life, he gravitated toward attractive, intelligent women. Fanny Wright had both qualities. This encounter confirmed his resolve to become a world reformer. Fanny Wright believed (in part due to the influence of Owen and Maclure) in the paramount necessity of religious and sexual emancipation as well as the emancipation of slaves. She had been duly excoriated by the New York *American* as a female monster.[16] Son Henry caustically remarks that "the Nashoba experiment failing, Fanny Wright sent her Negroes to Haiti and devoted her talents to the enlightenment of the American people and a war on marriage, property, and religion."[17]

Brownson *père* was enchanted. He had met a woman of "rare, original powers, and extensive and varied information" not to mention status. Fanny Wright was an intimate of General Lafayette and his family. She was also an acquaintance of Robert Owen and was associated with his son, Robert Dale Owen. In New York they published *The Free Enquirer*, the *New Harmony Gazette* in different costume. Brownson soon became a corresponding editor.[18] He later explained his cooperation with Wright and her associates as proceeding from his desire for truth. The characteristic American ambition, he expounded, is to attain practical truth, to know what ought to be done.[19]

The principal mover of his new enthusiasm was Fanny, attractive, forceful, a pleasing orator, at thirty "fresh and blooming with her feminine sweetness and her masculine intellect."[20] And Brownson had already been influenced in a more theoretical manner by Owen and Godwin. Godwin believed in progress and held that human nature was perfectible. Brownson studied his *Principles of Political Justice*, the same work that prodded Malthus to write *An Essay on the Principle of Population*. Although unable to swallow it whole, he contrasted Godwin's style favorably with that of Edmund Burke, stating that "it had more influence on my mind than any other book, except the Scriptures, I have ever read."[21] A typical Brownsonian dictum, it was the precursor of a lengthy parade of more or less outrageous statements. Owen's New Harmony community was designed to illustrate his "great principle" that education and environment mold human character. Even after the New Harmony experiment failed, it was considered the prototype of the later-to-be-completed masterwork.

Brownson admitted in retrospect that becoming a socialist was convenient. It provided a field for his activity, "devising, supporting, refuting, and rejecting theories and plans of world reform."[22] At the time he was not disturbed that this utopia could be realized only at the expense of property, marriage, and religion. Hindsight brought the realization that the plan was silly enough, and its success would make men well-trained and well-fed animals.[23] However, there may have been more to their activities than naive dilettantism. Both *Charles Elwood* and *The Table Rapper* suggest that the group was implicated, or at least believed itself to be implicated, in a conspiracy on the model of the Italian Carbonari. They aimed at obtaining control of the public school system and educating the children in a rational manner, which is to say, according to their dictates. The products of the system, "reasonable men," would shun the supernatural and fulfill their aspirations in this life, on this earth, by means of secular enterprises.

The little we know about this program suggests that it had all the marks of bland humanism. Its practical aspect, however, was more in keeping with the drift of nineteenth-century intrigue: obtain political power, co-opt the educational system, and transform humanity. Perhaps the otiose character of the enterprise arose, as Brownson suggested, from the absence of original philosophical foundations. Inspired by the popular philosophies of Locke and Condillac, the group drew their conclusion from the premises provided by the historical epoch and the country.[24] Brownson's enthusiasm for this ideology did not last, and his newly found "socialism" (at least its antireligious aspect) quickly receded. Brownson returned to religious belief...of a sort. This about face is depicted in *Charles Elwood*, a work that today seems diffuse and artificial, but was praised at the time by Edgar Allen Poe.

Brownson returned to the pulpit on the first Sunday of February 1831, at Ithaca, New York, and commenced editing and publishing a short-lived fortnightly, *The Philanthropist*. This was prompted by William Ellery Channing's sermon "Likeness to God," which Brownson praised extravagantly as the most remarkable sermon since the Sermon on the Mount.[25] It was a frank affirmation of the divinity of man and catapulted Channing into prominence and into the role of Brownson's mentor and father-figure. Brownson christened his resuscitated religious feelings "liberal Unitarianism." During his period of unbelief he had read Chateaubriand's *Génie du Christianisme* and absorbed the author's high regard for the works of French Catholic thinkers with liberal inclinations such as Lamennais, Lacordaire, and Montalembert. It was this movement above all else which brought him back to Christianity, inspiring him with belief in the possibility of reconciling modern society and religion, and inclining him toward a favorable appraisal of the Church.[26]

In the latter part of 1832 Brownson accepted a post as minister of a Unitarian congregation in Walpole, New Hampshire. Conscious to a painful degree both of his talents and negligible formal education, he began to read philosophy and study Latin, French, and German, all the while delivering four sermons a week and several Lyceum lectures. Italian and Spanish would be added later, and in 1844, classical Greek. His reading was voluminous, albeit idiosyncratic. But he became an educated man, a scholar in the accepted meaning of the word. As Maynard indicates, self-taught scholars were typical of his time. He cites Elihu Burritt, the learned blacksmith of Worcester, who mastered no less than forty foreign languages.[27] Brownson was a hard taskmaster, studying late into the night, relaxing by playing interminable games of chess.

Gifted with a capacious memory, Brownson retained most of what he read, often casting his thoughts into print before digesting them, using recently acquired material as fodder for the horse he was currently riding. He had a nose for ideas whose time had come. As Maynard notes, "hardly ever did he read a philosopher without making the claim that he had anticipated the idea."[28] If this is a flaw, it is at least in the grand tradition of Aristotle and Hegel, who considered that the best in prior philosophers had the merit of adumbrating their own thought. Brownson was not without self-esteem, even vanity. In a letter to his wife of October 15, 1829, he states that his Unitarian associates "are all respectable but with rather narrow views.... I have seen no one as yet that made me feel small.... My own conviction is that I am inferior only in useless browsing, but superior in practical knowledge."[29]

He visited Boston, meeting many leading Unitarians and the intellectual elite of the city, a notoriously closed set. While there, Brownson also met Channing and began a long friendship with George Ripley, acting editor of the *Christian Register*. He began a lengthy series of articles on several topics: French philosophers, Christianity, social progress, and so on. They appeared in Unitarian journals including the *Register*, the *Unitarian*, and the *Christian Examiner*. Brownson was invited to preach at leading congregations and lecture at centers such as the Masonic Hall and local Lyceums. Not only Fanny Wright, but other peripatetic would-be philanthropists such as Harriet Martineau were duly fascinated. Brownson's star was on the rise.

In spite of the waning of his socialist inclinations, Brownson retained a deep sympathy with the poorer and more numerous classes. He loathed modern industrialism as it had, in his opinion, reduced the great mass of workers to the level of slaves or worse, in many ways inferior to the Negro slaves in the Southern states. Democracy, though he favored it at this time, did not offer adequate protection to the working classes. In this, it was no more than an illusion.[30] His criticism was sharp and trenchant and his analysis of capitalism surprisingly acute. The same cannot be said of his aspirations, which merely echoed the aspirations of the French Revolution: to install heaven on earth.

Brownson was convinced that this goal could not be attained without the aid of religion. He later admitted that he had become a believer not in God but in humanity and had put humanity in the place of God.[31] He was fueled by the works of the French authors he had begun to read. Constant's lengthy *De la Religion Considérée dans sa Source, ses Formes et ses Développments* presented a theory explaining the development of religion that Brownson thought dovetailed with his own theory concerning human progress. Brownson was also influenced by the views of Saint-Simon and his disciples, especially those concerning property and the status of women. Property should be distributed according to merit. The complete equality of the sexes was advocated and patriarchal civilization condemned, as any institution founded solely by one of the two sexes must be woefully inadequate. Victor Cousin must be added to this list as he exercised a lengthy influence on Brownson, particularly through his key notion of eclecticism that Brownson quickly preempted and subjected to several variations.

He began to agitate for what he called the Church of the Future. This church would embody the advanced intelligence of the age and respond to those pressing needs and wants which humanity had developed over the past centuries. Though ostensibly settling for the supporting role of John the Baptist in the new dispensation, it is possible Brownson imagined himself in the principal role—a new Moses, a new Christ—a great man who, having internally realized the idea of the Church of the Future, could proceed to realize it externally.[32] These ideas were first articulated in a lengthy article, "New Views of Religion, Society, and the Church" (1834). Though not original in content, it was structured with typical Brownsonian panache. Concocting Churches of the Future was fast becoming a cottage industry. Brownson had previously shared his conception with Ezra Styles of Boston and Joseph Allen of Northborough. Based on Carlyle's *Sartor Resartus,* his article aimed at promoting the reunion of the scattered fragments of the Christian Church into a liberal, progressive institution. At Dedham, in his July 14 oration, Brownson touched on themes that would be incorporated into an agenda for the Church of the Future to be developed later. The declaration that "all men are created equal" was intended to extend further than simple political equality.[33] All inequity should fall under the ban.

Brownson and family moved to Canton, Massachusetts, and resided there for two years. George Ripley preached his sermon of installation. The service was attended by Adin Ballou. Brownson organized a Lyceum and established a small library. In the summer of 1835 he interviewed, and later hired, Henry Thoreau for a teaching post. They spent a "stimulating semester" together, studying German and chatting. (Some years later, Thoreau again appealed to Brownson for help. This time he was not successful. The self-proclaimed "frostbitten forked carrot" had previously been deficient in classroom regularity and evidenced many of the characteristics of a professional guest. They would reach their apogee in his relationship with Ralph Waldo Emerson.)[34]

By this time Brownson was identifying the spirit of Jesus with that of radical reform. He accordingly loosed a cannonade on all forms of inequality. Because of financial difficulties, the Brownsons, early in 1836, moved to Mount

Billington in Chelsea, a Boston suburb, and began to hold independent services in Boston.[35] In the autumn of that year a group, which included Brownson, met at Ripley's house. There they formed a society that would be called the Transcendentalist Club. This was a truly auspicious event.

II

Ego and Utopia

Of Brownson's early works, *Charles Elwood* and *New Views* are the most notable. The first was written in 1834 but not published until 1840; the second was published in 1836, the *annus mirabilis* of Transcendentalism. *Elwood* is a tedious and overembroidered account of a religious conversion, lacking verve and disfigured by maudlin touches. *New Views* is more successful, a manifesto rather than a treatise, direct and clear, in which the style calls for more substantial content. It elevated Brownson to public notice.

The first of three autobiographical efforts, *Charles Elwood* was possibly the least interesting. It lacked the crisp, informative narrative of *The Convert* or the intrigue and plunges into twilight esoterica of *The Spirit Rapper*. As one of the mirrors in which Brownson viewed himself while presenting himself to the public, it holds a certain interest in spite of its flaws. Charles Elwood, the protagonist, is the village infidel, the outsider, almost excluded from the human pale. An independent man, at odds with the public orthodoxy of the day, he endeavors to be authentic, to be always what he seems. He is—as Brownson believed himself to be—accompanied by a "glorious presence" and favored with "sweet and mysterious communion with the Father of man."[1]

There are three supporting characters—two probable Brownson surrogates and a female personality designed to evidence Elwood's sensitivity. At her death he whimpers, "I have planted wild flowers on her grave, and watered them with my tears."[2] The rest of the cast includes Mr. Wilson, a clergyman who views religion according to the dictates of Victor Cousin's philosophy, and Mr. Howard, perhaps Brownson's alter ego. Happily, the cardboard personalities and the feeble plot serve only as backdrops to his speculative muse, which, though hobbling, presents some interesting moves. Many of his later themes are found here *in ovo*. Present is the notion that God is known immediately through intuition, a theory he would later reinterpret in the light of Gioberti's philosophy. This would cause a good deal of mischief in the so-called ontologism controversy that became an albatross around his neck. Also present is the view that Christianity must be rectified and completed by means of a new church, a new Christ, and a new social order. He touches on other themes, even refurbishing arguments such as those found in Plato's *Euthyphro*, and concocts a demonstration of God's existence based on the Platonic ideas as interpreted by Cousin. There are a few surprises.

Though favorably impressed by Paley's *Natural Theology*, Brownson indicates that it was this argument that first raised doubts of God's existence in his mind. However, when the problem is attentively considered, it becomes clear that:

> No man does ever really deny the existence of God. Man may reject the term, but mean the reality. The existence of God is never proved, and never needs to be proved. All the atheist wants is to analyze his own faith, and whenever he does he will find God at the bottom.[3]

Brownson seems to be moving in an Anselmian mode (*Proslogion* 4) toward the novel solution later elaborated by C. S. Peirce with his notion of *musement*. This is a type of reflection, by means of which the idea of God's reality will be found an attractive fancy that can be developed by the muser. Peirce suggests that religious meditation be allowed to grow spontaneously out of what he calls pure play. This procedure causes a detachment by means of which the hypothesis that God exists will reach an almost unparalleled height.[4] Though Peirce's remarks tilt toward the subtle (a characteristic of which Brownson cannot be accused), one can be said to adumbrate the other, although Brownson's future attempts will take another route.

In *Elwood* he presents a demonstration in apparent contradiction with these assertions, based on the ideas of the Good, the True, and the Beautiful—Platonic ideas as interpreted by Cousin. Brownson affirms that these ideas have manifested themselves throughout the history of mankind as constituent elements of reason constantly struggling to realize themselves. However, unlike the Transcendentalist version, these ideas exist out of, not within, the human soul.[5] Man has a natural craving for these ideas, which he equates with the *Logos* or *Verbum*. This authenticates mankind's aspiration for the Infinite, the Godhead, of which the ideas are the facade. This craving for the Infinite is the religious sentiment, which is universal, eternal, and indestructible.[6] The ideas entail God in the same way that thought entails a thinker. Brownson believed this argument flowed from God's absolute necessity.[7]

But it is scarcely a rigorous demonstration. Brownson often becomes mesmerized by his own expertise in cranking out arguments that are often clear and forceful, but do not go as far as he would like. Yet, his is a valiant attempt if, as he believed, a demonstration consists in "stripping a subject of its envelopes, and showing it to reason as it is."[8] He will later return to this line of argument and attempt, with some success, to refine and strengthen it throughout his life.

For Brownson, abstract speculation goes hand in hand with political reform. The world is out of kilter. Society is unjust, an abomination: "the oppression of the toiling many to feed the luxury and vanity of the idle and worse than useless few, must be redressed."[9] While still influenced by Locke and relying on enlightened self-interest for purposes of reform, he took the plight of the poor masses with utmost seriousness. He was one of the few Transcendentalists who actually felt for the downtrodden, this perhaps because of his own background, reinforced by his social interpretation of the Scriptures. It was not merely a convenient pose. Aware that the elites fear crowds and hold the multitude in contempt, he viewed with suspicion any theory that would disinherit the masses and place them at the mercy of a select minority. Brownson contrasts the confidence of the elites in the masses' ability to be instructed by enlightened leaders (themselves) with their complete lack of confidence in the masses' ability to perceive the truth for themselves and act on it.[10]

At this point Brownson tilted toward an optimistic evaluation of human nature. He believed that all men were capable of perceiving the truth and acting on it as "the true light enlighteneth every man"(John 1:9). This light grounds the dignity of each individual. He was influenced by that Johannine derivative, the "inner light" of the Quakers, variations of which were found, in contemporary Transcendentalism. Unfortunately, the masses ignore their own dignity as they do the light within. While the Gospel aimed at making kings and priests of all men, elitism engendered the priesthood "and brought the human race into bondage to sacerdotal corporations."[11] Like Emerson and St. Augustine before him, Brownson urges men to turn their gaze inward to behold the light that is the source of inspiration. In a Hegelianesque turn, he indicates that when this light manifests itself in the masses, it is called the Spirit of the Age and is supernatural, divine.[12]

This displaces the focus of attention from the individual to the corporate. After writing *Elwood*, but prior to its publication, Brownson (influenced perhaps by Lammenais) developed his notion of the "American Idea," democracy, the equal rights and worth of every man as man.[13] He chastised Harvard College for its use of Locke as a required text since Locke's philosophy militated against the American Idea. The Church was duty bound to preach democracy, and Locke's thought disinherited the masses through its inherent undermining of liberty. He would later take Locke to task as one of the major provokers of the French Revolution.

Much attention is given to the notion of inspiration—which in his scheme of things is not only broad, but often confusedly so. Inspiration came to the biblical authors as flashes of lightning and manifests itself in the universal beliefs, the common notions of mankind, and in the ability possessed by all men to judge supernatural revelations. Brownson's notion of inspiration is difficult to comprehend because his early works present a conflation of the natural and supernatural, or at best a hazy delimitation of their respective domains. This may be due to the example of Transcendentalism and the prevailing speculative mist. Defined by Brownson as the spontaneous revelation of reason, his notion of inspiration is highly inclusive; David and Paul, Swedenborg, Penn, and Oberlin are all classed as prophets of God.[14]

Though he preaches a revolutionary Jesus and energetically advocates the Church of the Future, Brownson does not excoriate the existing churches, nor does he find them hateful.[15] Their doctrines are not false. They are defective. Each church professes a certain aspect of the truth while ignoring other equally essential aspects. Because of this, the Catholic Church, in its complete reality, cannot be identified with any of its external manifestations. He agreed with Emerson that the Christian churches had been structured according to the Jewish plan, a fundamental error.[16] Christianity should be the religion of the poor, but Roman Catholicism and Protestantism have set up authorities that deny this. They should be toppled.

In what may be a rationalistic move, Brownson admonishes the church to recognize the authority of pure reason, or "she will go the way of all the earth."[17] Although this strikes us as an appeal for religion within the limits of reason, it is actually a frank rejection of contingency. Like other Transcendentalists with revolutionary inclinations, he calls for a new Christ. Away with the old—the Jewish Christ, the son of Mary, clothed in flesh and subject to its infirmities. Proclaim "the new Christ, the Paraclete... the Spirit of Truth, who was to lead us into all Truth."[18] This is a strident, and to some extent vulgar sign of the times.

Perhaps his most novel view, one which tilts to the heterodox, is his notion of creation, which he views necessary since God cannot be what he is without creating. Although Brownson indicates that creation does not exhaust God and that His works are not necessary to His being, he still insists God is essentially a creator. Creation always was, though perhaps not in its present form.[19] In words that recall the Kabbalistic doctrine of *tsimtsum*[20] he postulates a God who creates not *ex nihilo* but out of Himself, out of His plenitude. The world, he states, "exists no further than He enters into it, and it ceases to exist... the moment he withdraws or relaxes the creative effort which brings it into being."[21] Obviously, this is not an exact reproduction; perhaps it is only a daring paraphrase of orthodox doctrine. However, it is certainly a tribute to Brownson's ingenuity and sensitivity to esoteric currents of thought.

Two years after the publication of *Elwood*, Brownson indicates that "the author has merely transferred to Charles Elwood his own experience as an unbeliever."[22] Even the unbeliever, as also the savage, has Christ at the bottom of his heart. He belongs to Christian civilization and "lives necessarily the life of Christ, so far as that civilization has realized it."[23] However, the civilized man is superior to the savage as the latter comes from an "inferior civilization" and is Christian in only a feeble sense. It is a question of degree, not of kind; Brownson emphasizes the importance of cultural background. A man is Christian only inasmuch as the civilization he inhabits is Christian.[24] While the Christian philosopher from a traditional civilization "thinks God," this is not true of the savage. The idea of God is attained only by successive efforts and repeated revelations.[25]

These speculations provide arguments in favor of Christianity as a religious and civilizational force. But they also may be viewed as an adumbration of the theory, lately in vogue, of the anonymous Christian. Brownson, at the end of *Elwood*, announces the appearance of his own philosophical system, an enterprise inaugurated in "Synthetic Philosophy."[26] This promissory note was never honored. In a last sally, Brownson deplores "the old stereotyped charge that we have changed our opinions again... [It]... has ceased to be musical and become somewhat monotonous and wearisome."[27] The accusation would continue to be voiced. It would continue to ring true.

New Views of Christianity, Society, and the Church placed
Brownson in the front ranks of the Transcendentalists and hit
a favorable note in the public consciousness. Though it revis-
its several topics explored in *Elwood,* many new ports of call
are added, due in part to the presence of Constant, Schleir-
macher, Saint-Simon, and Heine.[28] The religion natural to
man, "the sentiment of the holy," is no longer evidenced by
religious institutions that were far removed from the mind of
Jesus, who is the type, the model, of what religion should be.
All existing churches are at best imperfect representations.[29]
There are two antithetical systems disputing the primacy of
the world: Eastern Spiritualism and Western Materialism,
which reflect the opposition between spirit and matter. While
the church is placed in the category of spirit, reason and the
civil order are included under the category of matter. Yet, the
essential doctrine of Christianity states that there "is no
essential, no original antithesis, between God and man."[30]

The civil order should be subordinate to the religious,
Brownson argued, although the Church's exaggerated spiritualism has been an obstacle to efforts promoting well-being on
earth. This led to extravagances such as celibacy and promoted the caricature of the good Christian as a hermit
immured in a cave, counting beads, kissing his crucifix. Such
exacerbated spiritualism provoked a violent reaction from the
material order in the form of Protestantism, which generated
the modern state, civil liberty, human reason, philosophy,
industry—that is to say, all earthly endeavors.[31]

Under Protestantism, religion was subordinated to the
state, making philosophy a mixed blessing. Society has
rapidly moved toward unlimited freedom of thought, which
is to be feared, as limits are essential for civilization and
order. Man has moved from spiritualism, where philosophy is
an impossibility, to materialism, which deifies reason. The

necessary equilibrium between the spiritual and material orders has yet to be attained. Brownson contended that Protestantism lacks any religious character, although individual Protestants may retain a trace of religion, a residue of Catholicism. He believed Pelagianism, a naturalism severed from the supernatural, has become nearly universal.[32] It promotes civil and political liberty and prods the government in the direction of democratic forms: "liberty, not order, is the word that wakes the dead, and electrifies the masses."[33]

Protestantism is heading for a fall. Its situation resembles that of France during the Revolutionary era: the Church converted into the pantheon, God transmogrified into the symbol of human reason, man debased to the status of an automaton, signs of the triumph of materialism.[34] Unitarianism is the jumping off place for humanity to absolute infidelity. It is in decline while Roman Catholicism presents signs of revival. Nevertheless, Brownson applauds modernity and marks several of its advances. The rights of man are better secured than they ever were in Greece and Rome. Labor is accorded a certain dignity. The utter poverty that would again make man despair of the earth to seek refuge in dreams of the spirit-land is no longer possible. The urgent task at hand, given the flawed character of both exclusive spiritualism and exclusive materialism, is to reconcile matter with spirit. The Gospel has remained unfinished. It has yet to complete its work. Brownson asserts that "God has appointed us to build the New Church, the one that shall bring the whole family of man within its sacred enclosure," one that will successfully meld inspiration and philosophy.[35]

Unitarianism, in spite of its negative role of being Protestantism's last word before the deluge, enjoys the privilege of acting as the matrix of the doctrine of universal reconciliation. This is because it is the only religious body that bases religious faith on rational conviction.[36] All sects are drawn to this matrix. All churches are straining toward the constitution of this Church of the Future. Though less optimistic than Emerson and the more sanguine Transcendentalists, Brownson was an enthusiastic advocate both of progress and the United States' key role in the future advancement of humanity. In America, more than any other nation, the man of thought is united in the same person to the man of action, philosophical insight wedded to energetic, persevering activity. The time is not far distant, Brownson declares, "when our whole population will be philosophers, and all our philosophers will be practical men,"[37] a rather nice expression of American naiveté.

This reconciliation of spiritualism and materialism was accomplished, thought Brownson, through his theory of *Atonement*, by which both spirit and matter are pronounced as real and holy. If accepted, this doctrine would correct prevailing opinion regarding humanity, the world, and religion. We would remodel our institutions and eventually create a new civilization.[38] God's greatest gift to man is the ability to progress, an ability ingrained in human nature. The destiny of mankind, Brownson assures us, is "illimitable progress," "everlasting growth," and "the enlargement of being." The motto of the New Church, "Union and Progress," reflects this destiny and marks the task to be accomplished. This is a synthesis that the American people, because of their peculiar constitution, have the capacity to attain.

A trait of the American genius is that they put their speculative ideas to the test. Those ideas that prove true, can and will be realized.[39] This notion would be developed by C. S. Peirce and pass into American thought through "How to Make our Ideas Clear."[40] Among his contemporaries, Brownson considered that the exemplary synthesis of reason and inspiration was provided by William Ellery Channing. He applauds Channing's view that the doctrine of the God-Man substantiates the "homogeneousness" of the human and divine. All things are essentially holy.[41]

Six years after the publication of *New Views*, in his own review of the work, Brownson states that it marked a watershed: "it is upon the whole, the most genuine statement of our whole thought, of the principles which we believe must form the basis of the future church." [42] This statement comes in 1842, only two years before his conversion to Catholicism. He adds that it was written against those who believe that mankind has outgrown Christianity. This marks a retreat from his former position, perhaps caused by his increasing approximation to Catholicism. In any case, he insists that his views are in perfect harmony with the Gospel. The Incarnation has radiated throughout modern civilization. By restricting it to Jesus, the Church shows that it has not properly understood its true scope and, in effect, has disinherited the remainder of humanity. The New Church will not follow the Old Church in aiming at the sanctification of the individual, but will aim at the sanctification of humanity as a whole, an effort that might usher in an age of universal peace.[43] It is imperative to "generalize" the doctrine of the Incarnation. Spirit and matter must be united in actual life.

The Church of the Future will not be built on the ruins of the Old Church. Nor will it be the outgrowth of Protestantism, which preserves only dry forms and barren logic. As the fulfillment of the Old Church, the New Church will identify the service of God and the service of man: Church and State will be one.[44] Two grand conceptions act as the point of departure for this enterprise that aspires to "the brilliant conquest of the future."[45] They are Equality and Progress, which Brownson equates with the Incarnation of the *Verbum* in all men, already present in the mind of Jesus but only imperfectly articulated by the Church.

This revolutionary agenda, in which the turbulent emotions pulsating beneath the carapace of the logic-machine come to the surface, has points of similarity to some medieval speculations, including an attack on the supremacy of State over Church. Could this be a Comte-like attempt to establish the point of departure for his own Church in advance of the future? His penchant for tortured argumentation, fustian, and exaggeration often clouds the issue. To this may be added the exacerbations of his personality and his merciless pursuit of logical consistency.

Much is patchwork. Much is left unfinished. Often it is those ideas left in embryonic form that provide the most fruitful opportunities for future speculation. Brownson's intense religiosity has yet to be focused. He oscillates between piety and camp in the process of acquiring an intellectual deposit to give structure to his religious aspirations. Much of the rough Vermonter remains. When joined to a streak of imposture and quackery he is often unattractive. However, in Brownson we find a robust hardheadedness joined to intelligence, logical ability, and a gift for abstract thought which augurs better things to come. Though he often changes his views, this weather-cock will remain faithful to certain fundamental principles and attitudes that will come to constitute the scaffolding of his later thought and provide a storehouse for further speculation by future thinkers.

III

The Saturnalia
of Faith

As a member of the Transcendentalist Club, Brownson found himself part of a select, if motley, group that included such luminaries as Ralph Waldo Emerson, Amos Bronson Alcott, Theodore Parker, Henry David Thoreau, Margaret Fuller, William Henry Channing, and other notables of the day. The majority were Unitarian ministers, middle-class, Harvard educated, and unmarried. The average number of members during the years of its existence was about seventy. As Lewis Mumford nicely but inexactly stated, "in the act of passing away, the Puritan begot the Transcendentalist, and the will-to-power, which had made him what he was, with his firm but forbidding character, and his conscientious but narrow activity gave way to the will-to-perfection."[1] The transition was not as smooth as Mumford depicts. Unitarianism was a schism from Congregationalism, which was itself a schism from Calvinist Presbyterianism. Both Puritans (Calvinists) and Transcendentalists agreed that Congregationalism was a mere tissue of pale negations.[2]

In this milieu orthodoxy was identified with Genevan Calvinism as interpreted by the English divines of the Cromwellian period. Unitarians were distinguished from orthodoxy by their denial of the doctrines of the Trinity and

the divinity of Christ. Following Arminius, they held a more
optimistic notion regarding the status of man and of his ability to contribute to his own salvation; their optimism was
reflected in progressive views regarding the individual and
society.[3]

Unitarianism was the culmination of a tradition of protest
initiated by eighteenth-century ministers such as Chauncey,
Mayhew, and Freeman, who followed a philosophical orientation inspired by Locke. It was a sort of democracy. The
minister's authority was delegated by the congregation, which
possessed the authority even to alter doctrine. By 1825,
ninety-six orthodox churches had gone over to Unitarianism
which was also gathering adepts at Harvard.[4]

William Ellery Channing, whose sermon had so impressed
Brownson, was Unitarianism's greatest inspiration, while
Andrews Norton, Dexter Professor of Biblical Literature at
Harvard, was its chief orthodox opponent. Channing made a
serious attempt to resolve the question of authority—a question which deeply interested Brownson—by means of a
scheme of evidences that depended on Locke's epistemology
as interpreted by the Scottish school. It was heavily empiricist
and came increasingly under attack by the Transcendentalists,
for whom Locke was a favorite ogre. In any case, the question was imperfectly resolved.

It is not surprising that the name "Transcendentalism"
was at first unpopular. There were other names in the air:
"New School," "Symposium," "Disciples of Newness," even
the "Hedge Club," as meetings were arranged to coincide
with the visits of the Rev. Frederick Hedge of Bangor, Maine.
Emerson, with his customary panache, called it "a Saturnalia
of Faith," tartly observing that the view of Transcendentalism
on State Street is that it threatens to invalidate contracts.[5]
Brownson opted for "eclecticism," but "Transcendentalism"

won the day. It was a loosely connected, rather bizarre, group, made more bizarre by later historians who have not hesitated, according to inclination, to read out of their ranks some of their most illustrious members including Brownson, Alcott, Parker, and even Emerson.[6]

What did the members of the Club have in common? Primarily, a tilt toward intuition, optimism, utopianism, and social reform. Russell Kirk speaks of an expansive New England conscience that expressed itself in misty optimism, social experimentation, and metaphysical creations;[7] but he was scarcely an admirer. Octavius Brooks Frothingham, in his bombastic apologia for the Transcendentalists, traces its principles to Kant, Jacobi, and Fichte. However, their thought reached America principally through the medium of literary fellow travelers: Goethe, Richter, and Novalis as interpreted by Carlyle, Coleridge, and Wordsworth.[8] In addition, as indicated by Perry Miller, the roots of Transcendentalism can also be traced back to native origins, among others to the doctrine of emanation put forward by Jonathan Edwards.[9] Henry Hedge was the only member of the Club who had been educated in Germany. Many Americans felt, as did Professor Felton of Harvard, that "German metaphysics and philosophical religion make me feel like a mouse under an air pump."[10]

As previously noted, this Teutonic mist reached the United States principally through English interpreters. Orestes Brownson contributed to this invasion by writing some papers praising Carlyle. John Beezier, a Harvard professor, was disturbed by this and remarked that "his admirers belong to the class of persons who were endangering the morals of the community."[11] The critique was misplaced as Brownson, due to his massive project of self education, was one of the few Transcendentalists able not only to handle abstract theory but actually to relish the enterprise. This was especially the case with French thinkers such as Cousin, Royer-Collard, and Maine de Biran. In 1836, Brownson reviewed three of Cousin's books, suggesting that his eclecticism might prove useful in ending the "war" between religion and philosophy. Ripley was impressed while Emerson was dismayed.[12]

The Transcendentalists were, as Frothingham notes, Protestants of the most intellectual type. Catholicism was decidedly marginal: "none besides the Irish laboring and menial class were Catholic and their religion was considered as the lowest form of ceremonial superstition."[13] While Catholicism was dismissed out of hand, the pale negations of Unitarianism failed to satisfy, as did the strict Calvinism of orthodoxy. Along with others, Emerson reacted against historical Christianity, balking at administering Holy Communion, finally resigning his ministry in October 1832. Others followed his example.

The official organ of the Club was *The Dial*, which during its tenure of less than four years (July 1840–April 1844) provides clues to the brief but eventful existence of Transcendentalism. Emerson and Margaret Fuller debuted as editors. *The Dial* featured chapters of "Ethical Scriptures" which, at one time or other, included texts from Confucius, Hermes Trismegistus, the Chaldean Oracles, and other esoterica. *Dial* readers encountered Plato with the aid of Thomas Taylor, a British scholar of Neoplatonic bent, while they dabbled in more exotic fare: Swedenborg, Boehme, and Eastern classics such as the *Bhagavad Gita*.[14] Brownson was not a contributor. Nevertheless, Emerson was so delighted with Brownson's incendiary "The Laboring Classes" (1840), that he wrote Margaret Fuller: "the hero wields a sturdy pen.... Let him wash himself and write for the immortal *Dial*."[15]

How did Brownson fare among these New England mandarins? Frothingham, writing in 1876, may have captured some of their discomfort in dealing with this unkempt outsider when he writes that Brownson was

> a remarkable man, remarkable for intellectual force and... intellectual willfulness... his mind was restless, audacious, swift; his self-assertion was immense, his thought came in floods... no rational stability of principle, an experimenter in systems... an extraordinary man.[16]

He was clubbable only with difficulty, looking with disfavor on certain Transcendentalist fads such as the practice of dietetics. While firmly anti-slavery, he did not share their passion for abolition. He took a distance from those utopian projects that refused to accept man as he is but attempted to fabricate a caricature in accordance with their whims.

Fruitlands and Brook Farm were Transcendentalist projects. Fruitlands was an Alcott enterprise. Meat, alcohol, tea, coffee, and milk were forbidden, as were potatoes that did not grow toward the sun. Added to the list were woolen and cotton garments as they were the products of slavery.[17] Much of this seems to adumbrate the distorted quasi-Puritanism of a later date. But Transcendentalists also shared a feeling that America was a country of beginnings—of, as Mumford states, vast designs and expectations, holding out the promise of an unspotted nature and a fresh start.[18] This was leavened by a pronounced streak of hokum that Brownson shared with his peers, though to a lesser degree.

They were a motley group. The ethereal Emerson and the incessant chatterer Bronson Alcott, author of *Orphic Sayings*. Margaret Fuller, as sharp-tongued as she was ugly, a superb literary critic and unrelenting activist. Theodore Parker, "our Savonarola," the diminutive, fiery preacher and nebulous thinker. George Ripley, the mild, idealistic translator of Cousin's *Philosophical Miscellanies*, founder of Brook Farm, and, of the group, Brownson's closest friend. Henry David Thoreau, enthusiast, naturalist, eccentric, caustic wit, who lived for six weeks with the Brownsons and taught school at Canton. Amos Perry, a friend of Thoreau's at Harvard, let drop two surprising remarks: that Thoreau spoke of Brownson with greater admiration than for any other writer and that his profound love of nature was inspired by Brownson and not Emerson.[19]

Viewed from the Roman Catholic perspective that Brownson would later adopt, the Transcendentalists were a chamber of horrors. Emerson believed that the works of Plato and Mohammed were as inspired as Scripture. Theodore Parker awaited the coming of a new avatar, superior to Jesus, while Margaret Fuller called for a life more complete and various than that of Christ. Thoreau excoriated churches as the ugliest buildings in any village as they are places "in which human nature stoops the lowest and is most disgraced."[20]

Several members of the Club were infatuated with Greek classicism or lured by Eastern esoterica. Thoreau declares, "in my Pantheon, Pan still reigns in his pristine glory" while also speaking of "seemingly unimportant and unsubstantial things... [such as]... Father, Son, and Holy Ghost."[21] An exponent of the rugged life and denizen of Walden Pond, he contended that a healthy man, with steady employment, would not be a good subject for Christianity.[22] Yet even Thoreau falls into the Transcendentalist penchant for misty romanticism. He is granted a quasi-mystical experience, "a surge of vast, titanic, inhuman, nature" on the summit of modest Mount Katahdin.[23] Transcendentalists enjoyed transmuting the pedestrian into high drama.

Transcendentalism did not emerge from a vacuum. It was much more than a stew of speculative chestnuts taken from the European hearth. Nor was it merely an intellectualistic pose, though it doubtless was also that. To begin with, Transcendentalism was creative. It sparked a movement that would generate an American literature of major proportions. Moreover, as David Bowers has indicated, although their vocabulary was borrowed from European thought, the appropriation of certain insights of Puritan, Quaker, and other colonial theologies, refracted through the secular and egalitarian ideology of the revolution, must also be taken into account.[24] He maintains that Transcendentalism owed its pervasive moralism to Puritanism, the "inner light" and the concept of intuition to the Quakers, and the belief that the individual enjoys immediate access to divine truth. To Unitarianism it owed the double reduction of God to a universal principle and this principle to man. It also adopted their rejection of the supernatural and sin. Finally, Transcendentalism owes its religious enthusiasm to Jonathan Edwards.[25] The microcosm holds the key to the mysteries of the macrocosm. Man is the privileged center and door to the universe. Knowledge begins with self-knowledge.

Charles Dickens, in his *American Notes*, observed: "I was given to understand that whatever was unintelligible would certainly be transcendental," adding that the Transcendentalists "are followers of my friend Mr. Carlyle, or I should say, of a follower of his, Mr. Ralph Waldo Emerson.... If I were a Bostonian I think I would be a transcendentalist."[26] Oddly enough, at this time Emerson was busy describing a meeting of the Friends of Universal Reform, an offshoot of Transcendentalism. It was a picaresque assembly. According to the sage it included "madmen, madwomen, Dunkers, Muggletonians, Groaners, Quakers, Abolitionists, Unitarians, Philosophers, and others… the faces were a study."[27] One wonders if Emerson considered this kaleidoscopic assemblage a worthy expression of the Oversoul? Did the participants realize that they were experiencing the American dream at its moment of greatest intensity and innocence?

Transcendentalism's *bête noire* was John Locke whose philosophy was dominant in clerical circles and academic institutions. It was usually identified as sensationalism and included additions and modifications from Scottish Common Sense philosophy. Brownson stated in 1839 that "all the leading French infidels, they who did the most to overturn the Church and prepare the Reign of Terror, were disciples of Locke and Anglomaniacs."[28] Locke's *Essay* was a well-studied textbook at most New England colleges: Yale, Harvard, Dartmouth, and Brown.[29] This was unacceptable to many influential clerics. Marsh believed that "sensational philosophy" was the main reason for the woeful absence of spiritual content in contemporary religion. This view gained ground in certain circles to the point where Locke became identified with everything objectionable in Unitarianism. The reaction against Locke, in which Brownson was to participate, centered on man's ability to transcend experience and achieve direct contact with truth, or to become, in Emerson's phrase, a transparent eyeball.

Locke has no shortage of champions. Prominent men such as Edward Everett, Leonard Withington, and Francis Bowen fought back. Bowen marked Transcendentalism as "abstruse in its dogmas, fantastic in its dress, and foreign in its origin."[30] He chided their obsession with phraseological innovation, their obscurity of thought, philosophical naivete, and lack of coherence. This paved the way for the most notorious blast against Transcendentalism, Andrews Norton's *A Discourse on the Latest Form of Infidelity.*

At this time the Jacksonians, as Arthur Schlesinger indicates, were carrying out a revolt in the political realm analogous to that of the Transcendentalists in the religious.[31] However, the move toward egalitarianism did not have major resonance in Transcendentalist circles, at least on a practical level, as only Orestes Brownson and George Bancroft were really committed to the struggle. Schlesinger notes with evident distaste that the majority "from their book-lined studies or their shady walks in cool Concord woods... found the hullabaloo of party politics unedifying and vulgar."[32] Although Emerson enthusiastically supported the move toward egalitarian democracy, he remained cautious and aloof. This was possibly due to his well-grounded fear of institutions, but there might also be other, deeper reasons: his distaste for concrete existence, for time and history, for any obstacle that impeded the leap of the mind into the immutable eternal.

Henry James acutely observed that certain chords of Emerson's personality were wholly absent—great chunks of literature, art and music were hidden to his gaze—and faulted him for lack of color, for giving a singular impression of paleness.[33] Several Club members shared this characteristic. With all their zest for reform and aspiration to utopia there is a marked absence of a realistic sense of evil. Brownson was the exception. Hedge perceived in him the combative vigor of Transcendentalism.[34] In 1836, the *annus mirabilis* of the group, Emerson, published *Nature,* Alcott, the first volume of *Conversations on the Gospels,* Convers Francis, *Christianity as a Purely Internal Principle,* and Brownson, *New Views.* When *Nature* was attacked, Orestes Brownson came resolutely to its defense in spite of the fact that he believed that Emerson had gone too far: that his thrusts against historical Christianity were too extreme and that Emerson's notion of obedience to self amounted to the deification of the soul with a vengeance.[35]

In 1841, Brownson summed up his then largely favorable opinion of Transcendentalism in *The Dial*:

> To our taste they lack robustness, manliness, and practical aims. They are too vague, evanescent, aerial, but nevertheless... one cannot help feeling that these are after all the men and women who are to shape our future.[36]

Four years later, he takes a more negative view. Transcendentalism is "the last stage on this side of nowhere, the logical and historical evolution of Protestantism." It is the Gospel turned upside-down and exalts the inferior soul, the seat of concupiscence, placing it above man's spiritual nature. The Transcendentalists are not reasoners, but "seers" who believe that passion and imagination are superior to reason. Brownson grumbles: "we will not believe them till they tell us what they see."[37]

IV

The Aeolian Harp

Ralph Waldo Emerson was the avatar, the prophet, of Transcendentalism. This paradigmatic New Englander (who seemed to walk on stilts), the offshoot of a race of ministers, was eccentric, charming, and able to captivate even rude Western ranchers with his nasal pontifications. *Nature*, published in 1836, can be considered the charter of Transcendentalism—a judicious combination of bombast, sentiment, psychological insight, and philosophical muddle. This *mélange*, spiced by intimations of paradise regained, gave Emerson a special niche in both American letters and the American psyche. Walking in the woods, he is transformed into a transparent eyeball: "I am nothing. I see all; the currents of universal being circulate through me; I am a part or particle of God."[1] The gospel he would preach for more than four decades is here found in ovo. The presence of Plato, and to some extent Hegel, will be in evidence but their thought is refracted through the very peculiar mirror of Emerson's mind.

Nature is the symbol of the spirit, the vehicle of thought; words are signs of natural facts. Nature is allied to religion and with it subordinated to morality, that ethical character that penetrates nature, and is "the pith and marrow of every substance, every relation, and every process."[2] This is an exquisite but fragile conception. Emerson admits that it is doubtful whether nature possesses substantial existence. Nevertheless, though it exists only "in the apocalypse of the mind," nature is no less useful and venerable.[3] While the "sensual man" conforms his thought to things, the idealist, the poet, conforms things to his thought. He appreciates that nature is plastic and so impresses his being on it.[4] As with most thinkers of the Platonic tradition, Emerson aspires to apprehend—to grasp—those ideas or absolutes that are immortal, necessary, and uncreated natures, and in so doing, to exist authentically. Ethics and religion are the means by which these ideas are incorporated into life, and by which the soul can ascend to them.[5] This centrality of the ideas diminishes the reality of the physical world and the luster of the contingent as it is evidenced in persons, history, and miracles. The ability of man to come in contact with the ideas illustrates his infinite possibilities: he is the creator in the finite. However, man is not aware of his own dignity as he is alienated, severed from his true self. Emerson urges, "all that Adam had, all that Caesar could, you have and can do.... Build, therefore, your own world."[6]

The humanism, moralism, tilt to the intuitive, and frank distaste for the concrete found in Nature is echoed in his 1838 address to the Senior Class in Divinity College, Cambridge. He indicates that human insight into moral sentiment is not subject to time, space, and circumstance, that it authenticates the soul's elevated status. This "divine impulse" does not proceed from Western civilization but from the Orient. Like the early Hegel of *The Spirit of Christianity*, Emerson views Jesus Christ as testifying to the greatness of man: "He is the only soul in history who has appreciated the worth of a man."[7] Historical Christianity has fallen into a grievous error attended by a multiplicity of evils by exaggerating the personal (of Jesus), the positive, and ritualistic. This corrupts and vitiates any effort to communicate religion. Because of this error, we are today dealing with a decaying church and wasting unbelief.[8]

Like other Transcendentalists, Brownson included, Emerson proclaimed the need for a "new revelation," a "true Christianity," which proclaims a Christ-like faith in the infinitude of man: "dare to love God without mediator or veil."[9] Traditional Christianity, with its Jewish roots, is hardly to his liking. Although the Hebrew and Greek Scriptures contain immortal sentences, they possess no special integrity. A new Teacher is necessary, one who understands that the world is the mirror of the soul.[10] Unlike Brownson, whose efforts in the direction of the Church of the Future did not sever him radically from traditional Christianity, Emerson carried the demythologization of Christianity to its radical extreme by practically deifying man while succumbing to the vague and vast speculations coming from the Orient.

Further dimensions of Emerson's thought are encountered in "The Transcendentalist," a lecture given at the Boston Masonic Temple in January 1842. What is the premier transcendentalist's reading of Transcendentalism? Very simply, it is Idealism as it is found in 1842. Opposed to Realism, which insists on facts, circumstance, and history, the Idealist stresses the power of thought and will, i.e., inspiration. Mind is the only reality. The world is merely an appearance. Emerson flirts with antinomianism and appeals to the East, in particular, Buddhism.[11] In one of those superb phrases that almost topples into the absurd, he speaks of Transcendentalism as "the Saturnalia or excess of Faith, the presentiment of a faith proper to man in his integrity."[12] Paradise is in the process of being stormed.

Emerson's portrait of the Idealist/Transcendentalist tilts toward the fussy and prissy. He is a man who is solitary and fastidious, a worshiper of beauty, repelled by vulgarity and frailty, not a good citizen or upstanding member of society. He pleads: "will you not tolerate one or two solitary voices in the land speaking for thoughts and principles not marketable and perishable?"[13] Then, as now, commercial hubris has often exercised a harmful influence on American society. Emerson's plea cannot be dismissed as the whimper of an effete intellectual.

The ninth essay of Emerson's *First Series*, "The Over-Soul," is one of his most abstract (some would say inane, others, inspirational) pieces. Granting the assumption that man is a stream fed by a hidden source, Emerson attempts to describe this fountainhead that contains the particular being of each individual as well as the principle of unity of all particulars. This is the Over-Soul, "the common heart... the Eternal One."[14] A good case can be made that the Over-Soul is one of the latest variations, one of the last of an extended list, of Aristotle's *poietikon* (Activity) as interpreted by Alexander and taken up by Islamic philosophers such as Avicenna. Under the name of the Agent Intellect it cut a large swath in medieval speculation. With Emerson it is carrying Hegelian, Spinozan, and Oriental accretions.

Emerson pictures the Over-Soul bursting through the facade of the Temple (man): "When it breathes through his intellect, it is genius; when it breathes through his affection, it is love; when it breathes through his will, it is virtue."[15] The Over-Soul is impersonal. It gives itself by passing into and becoming the man it enlightens. Emerson calls these privileged experiences "announcements" or "manifestations." This influx of the Divine Mind into the human is attended by the emotion of the sublime, enthusiasm, which can run the gamut from the faintest glow to the heights of ecstasy.[16] He inverts the "look within" of the Augustinian tradition. The self is not the medium of access to God; nor is prayer a means of muting the chaotic impulses that arise through concupiscence. On the contrary, prayer, worship of God, is a penetration within the self. Worship becomes self-worship:

> I am born into the great, the universal mind. I, the imperfect, adore my own perfect.... More and more the surges of everlasting nature enter into me, and I become public and human in my regards and actions.[17]

Much of Emerson's Transcendentalism is autobiography. "New England Reformers" is a case in point. He excoriated contemporary education as artificial, cosseted, and parochial, a constant struggle against common sense.[18] It is imperative to discard the superfluous and develop the self-supplied powers of the individual. There must be faith in man, especially when, in the opinion of many, society is viewed as a hospital for incurables. In spite of many indications to the contrary, "there is a power over and behind us, and we are the channels of its communications."[19] The man who advances only by obedience to his genius testifies to the presence of the Over-Soul.[20]

For a person who enjoys contrasting sheep and goats, the good and bad—perhaps a legacy from his Puritan ancestors—Emerson is singularly devoid of a vivid sense of evil. He asserts that when the conservative (evil) ethos prevails men are at their least vigorous and most luxurious. When the radical (good) prevails then the mind is aroused when music is heard and poetry read. The huddled masses are left out in the cold as the many conflicts with his ideal of self-reliance.

Though theoretically inclined to Utopianism, he was wary of utopian communities of a popular stripe as they "promise to become an asylum to those who have tried and failed, rather than a field for the strong."[21] Emerson had a predilection for the strong.

In terms that could hardly be equaled by the most reactionary conservative, Emerson voices his contempt of the masses: "enormous populations, if they be beggars, are disgusting, like moving cheese, like hills of ants, or of fleas... the more the worse." However, he adds the amusing admonition given the context: "we must not... deny the substantial existence of other people."[22] Nevertheless, Nature exists for the excellent and is an obstacle to the masses. Nature is a "brilliant core" emitting sparks; each spark is the carrier of a new secret. However, Emerson can state "there are no common men" in a fit of transcendental egalitarianism while pontificating from the heights about the poor Paddy, whose country is his wheelbarrow, and can ask "Why are the masses, from the dawn of history down, food for knives and powder?"[23]

There is no contradiction. Persons are simply unimportant to Emerson. He praises the individual repeatedly but he is valuable primarily as the carrier of quality of the Over-Soul: "the men who exhibit them have now more, and less, and pass away; the qualities remain on another brow."[24] Great men exist to produce greater men. Emerson aspires to vault above the physical realm of contingency and the spiritual realm of personhood to reach the World of Ideas, the core of the Over-Soul. In a nice variation on the Platonic doctrines of participation he contends that the transient world can be said to exist only in the measure that it reflects the Ideas. Emerson's notion of intuition resembles Platonic recollection with the great men acting as the vehicles for the Ideas and the point of departure for the mind's leap into itself.

When Emerson writes on Plato, he is perceptive and only slightly nebulous. Few highly bizarre interpretations are encountered: one of these is converting Plato into an American genius.[25] Universality can be pushed too far. On the whole his vision is clear. Emerson fingers unity and diversity as the two cardinal principles that ground Plato's philosophy. Thought tends to unity, activity to diversity. Metaphysics and Natural Philosophy, which express the genius of Europe, represent variety and rest on the religion of Asia (unity).[26] As dialectic is grounded on the observation of identity and diversity so as to discern between the true and false, it is lauded as "the science of sciences."[27] Plato, in Emerson's estimation, is the great average man, a genius of equilibrium in whom men can visualize their own dreams and possibilities. In a nasty aside, he indicates that Plato's only flaw is that his writings are not accorded "the vital authority which the screams of the prophets and the visions of unlettered Arabs and Jews possess."[28]

The fanciful, precious, grandiose, and esoteric—traits that Emerson cultivated to fine brilliance—are illustrated in "Swedenborg; or, the Mystic." Often his enthusiasm lapses into plain silliness, as when he states, "the genius was to penetrate the science of the age with a far more subtle science: to pass the bounds of space and time; venture into the dim spirit-realm, and attempt to establish a new religion in the world."[29] One finds sparks of unintentional humor as when he credits Swedenborg with the merit of mass and refers to him as "one of the missouriums and mastodons of literature."[30] Emerson believed Swedenborg was attempting to remedy the appalling situation of the withered traditional church by letting in nature and attempting to extract universal meaning from the literal. However, this attempt was flawed because of Swedenborg's attachment to Christian principle rather than to moral sentiment. Emerson takes him to task for his denial of the conversion of evil spirits, the often illusory character of his revelations, and his obsession with filth and corruption.[31]

However, because of the strength of Swedenborg's intellect, Emerson considered him the last Father of the Church.[32] This is not meant facetiously. The age was attracted to monumental humbugs, some worse by far than the Scandinavian mystagogue. Brownson was no exception. Neither was his friend, Father Hecker, who collected a veritable menagerie of eccentric acquaintances. Unsettlement was in the air. The search for a new Christ, for a resuscitated Joachite Dux, had muddied the waters. Emerson can exclaim:

> The world still wants its poet-priest, a reconciler who shall not trifle with Shakespeare the player, nor shall grope in graves with Swedenborg the mourner; but who shall see, speak and act, with equal inspiration.[33]

Emerson was singularly blind to contingency and evil. He despised both historical Christianity and convention as both are grounded on a temporal existence and historical situation. He believed that every great figure is disconnected from contingency and produces a rupture. Nature intervenes through these great men to oppose convention and reveal it to be the chimera that it, in fact, is. Sin, which is made possible by contingency, is denied or bracketed. Russell Kirk saw the consequences of such a position when he stated that Emerson was the most powerful apologist of the ostrich-tendency of the American people.[34] If Kirk is right, it would appear that the dragon's teeth sown by Emerson and the Transcendentalists came to produce a bitter harvest.

Undergirding Emerson's often insightful and witty views runs the current of a master theme larded by a vein of resentment. He marks Napoleon as selfish, perfidious, unscrupulous, and singularly destitute of generous sentiments. Goethe is belittled as the amateur of all arts, sciences, and events. Yet he considers them "two stern realists, who... have severally set the axe at the root of the tree of cant and seeming."[35] In "English Traits," a lengthy catalogue of Emerson's views on the English, both the positive and the negative are frankly, even tartly, stated. The English are sincere, have the finest women in the world, and a church notable for grace and good sense. No doubt, "England is the best of the actual nations."[36] They are censored for "the habit of brag," are resistant to change, possess little if any imagination, have cold and repressive manners, and "have lost all commanding views in literature, philosophy and science."[37] However, though the English are slow, staid and sad by comparison to the singing and dancing nations, compared to Americans they are content and cheerful.

His distaste for the Irish must have been compounded by his experiences in England. The Irish are the degenerate *doppelganger* of the English: poor, politically dependent, a misplaced race. Irish members of Parliament enjoy a poor reputation because of their woeful lack of character. Emerson, when he visited the Irish districts, found them populated by "men deteriorated in size and shape, the nose sunk, the gums exposed, with diminished brain and brutal form."[38] There are similar passages in other works.[39] When Brownson's role in the Nativist controversy is discussed, it should be viewed within the context of such demeaning views, which were hardly restricted to Emerson or the Transcendentalists.

Emerson's depiction of the U.S. as seen from across the pond, perhaps in part for English consumption, is attractively alien, nearly surrealistic. It is a world that has in most part vanished:

> In America lies nature sleeping, over-growing, almost conscious, too much by half for man in the picture, and giving a certain tristesse, like the rank vegetation of swamps and forests seen at night... and on it a man seems not able to make much impression.[40]

It is a different world from the trim hedgerows and cultivated gardens of England. When asked whether there were any autochthonous American ideas, Emerson replied: nonresistance and the dogma of non-government.[41]

There are acute observations and happy phrases. The English avoid anything marked. Enthusiasm is permitted only in the opera. Their capital institution is dinner. The religion of England forms a part of good breeding: "by taste are ye saved."[42] Anglicanism is the religion of the Old Testament, the religion of the pound sterling. Neither Transcendentalist nor Christian, "they are stagnant and the new age has new desires, new enemies, new trades, new charities, and reads the Scriptures with new eyes."[43] Emerson takes great satisfaction in claiming that both St. George and Amerigo Vespucci were knaves, frauds, and imposters: "We are equally badly off in our founders."[44]

Emerson's thought was a distillate, a splendid distillate, intellectually radicalized, of American Public Orthodoxy, at least of its New England branch. We find dislike of tradition, infatuation with the new and the esoteric, puritanical moralism, preciosity, utopianism, and a strong undercurrent of resentment. These traits have perdured to some extent until the present and periodically rise to the surface. Today they are

greatly tarnished and have become wearisome. In Emerson
they were accompanied by unusual, perhaps extraordinary,
talents. It is virtually impossible to dislike him, that venerable
tintype of the glorious proboscis. He was too detached, too
self-absorbed, too reserved, to provoke authentic hostility. At
Longfellow's funeral, Emerson is reported to have said: "that
gentleman was a sweet, beautiful soul, but I have entirely forgotten his name."[45] There we may see him slipping down the
garden path to senility. A finale more in character and certainly more reflective of his thought would have been the last
words of Vespasian as reported by Suetonius: "Vae. I must be
turning into a God."

In Brownson's America Emerson was a gigantic figure
who was bound to influence and be emulated. There are lyri-
cal passages in the early Brownson (mostly unfortunate) that
are clearly Emersonian, and fit the author, as badly as a lace
peignoir fits a bear. Although Brownson was not impressed
by Emerson as a philosopher, his tone, and the atmosphere
that pervaded Transcendentalism, largely Emersonian, influenced him greatly. Even the vicissitudes of Brownson's post-
conversion life, in which he opposed Transcendentalism,
could not eradicate the traces of this early enthusiasm.
Though Brownson rejected certain major tenets of Transcendentalism and moved away from its social and political manifestations, its spirit pursued him to the end. Throughout his
later life we witness the return of the repressed, incorporated
into some of Brownson's most novel speculations.

V

Social Radical

Orestes Brownson made a forceful attempt to put his socio-religious imperative to work in the practical order when he founded The Society for Christian Union and Progress. It advocated free inquiry, a strict code of morality, and the amelioration of the lot of the poorest and most numerous class. The Reformation, he believed, had introduced an era of revolution and destruction that had been carried far enough. It was time to begin the work of reconstruction, to build the scaffolding necessary to construct the Church of the Future. This summons to action was not taken seriously in some quarters. Carlyle remarked to Theodore Parker that these "new views" were as old as Voltaire and joked about Brownson[1]—hardly the respect merited by the self-professed third most profound man in America. Carlyle was right. Much of Brownson's thought at this early date was scarcely original. The "Religion of Progress" certainly is not and *New Views*, a manifesto setting forth the mission of the Society and presenting his irenic vision of "shining new synthesis" of the partial truths of past churches was, at least in conception, somewhat moth-eaten.

However, Brownson's manner of exposition held the attention of the public. He was direct, forceful, logical, proceeding directly from his belief that Jesus' thought coincided perfectly with democracy. The substance of his preaching for some ten or eleven years was constituted by a sort of Christian Democracy inspired in part by Saint-Simon.[2] Henry Brownson, his son and editor, observes that "many supposed him to be a visionary, but the general belief was that he excited the poor against the rich."[3] Brownson himself believed that his "plan" had been revealed to him by a flash of inspiration.[4] In a letter to Bancroft (Sept. 25, 1836) he states, "You are but following out the direction which modern civilization is to bring. All things tend to democracy. Those who support it are sure of the future.... I am trying to democratize religion and philosophy."[5]

The Panic of 1837 spurred his prophetic enthusiasm. In May of 1837, Brownson delivered a sermon on "The Fall of the Spirit of Gain" in which he demanded "not equal wealth but equal chances to wealth."[6] On July 4 he spoke at the Democratic mass meeting at Bunker Hill. Later that month, in *The Reformer*, he attacked the belief that the interests of the poor coincide with those of the rich.[7] He was himself attacked for his views as unChristian and blasphemous. It was reported that he had professed atheism and had savaged the clergy, calling them infidels. Miss Elizabeth Peabody communicated these rumors to Brownson, observing, "I was present at the sermon, and with those around me, was very much affected and stirred up by the glowing faith in Christ, which so strongly pervaded it."[8]

On the political front he allied himself with Bancroft and the Democratic Party. He perceived the Whig Party, solidified by the 1837 Panic, as a threat to popular liberties. Bancroft, appointed Collector of the Port of Boston (1836), named Brownson as steward of the U.S. Marine Hospital at Chelsea (1838) at a salary of $1,600 per annum. (He also appointed

Nathaniel Hawthorne to the Custom House at a salary of $1,500.) In December of 1837 Brownson launched the *Boston Quarterly Review* as editor and major contributor. It proposed to Christianize democracy and democratize the church, to ground theology in philosophy, and elevate labor. Thoreau wrote that he had read the first number of the *Review* and liked the spirit of independence that distinguished it, adding that "it is high time that we knew where to look for the expression of American thought."[9] About a century later, Harold Laski spoke of the *Boston Quarterly Review* and *Brownson's Quarterly Review* (established 1844) as astonishing, indicating that the former enjoys permanent significance in American intellectual history.[10] Brownson early considered that the American people had a providential mission; they were a chosen people to whom the constitution of the Church of the Future was committed. He believed that this would lead to a global new order.

Although a radical democrat, Brownson was ill at ease with any deification of the masses, of public opinion. In "Democracy," he insists that the state must be limited by justice. This will prevent the multiplicity of evils that necessarily follow from defining Right by public opinion.[11] Inspired by John C. Calhoun, the "providential man," Brownson advocates States Rights as a guarantee of freedom, remaining an eccentric Democrat in whose thought religion and politics were conflated.[12] He expects that the present "monarchy of the bourgeoisie" would ultimately be replaced by the "monarchy of humanity." Conceptions of this sort had been in the air for some time and had been taken up, some would say with a vengeance, by several American thinkers. George Bancroft, in a letter of Sept. 21, 1836, asks Brownson if he had read Vico. The postscript notes that "the day for the multitude has now dawned."[13]

He chastised both Northern industrialism and the abolitionists, whose antics, he believed, served to distract the public's attention from truly important matters. No doubt, slavery was morally wrong. But it was no worse than Northern wage-bondage, even superior to it in some ways. The violent tactics of the abolitionists, applauded by Thoreau and even by Emerson after a period of indecision, could, in Brownson's opinion, easily be converted to the service of despotism. History may have proved him to be right. His analysis of capitalism was surprisingly on target. Schlesinger indicates that "his brilliant historical analysis makes the class struggle the dynamic force in the evolution of society."[14] It placed under siege that very center of Whig ideology, around which all else revolves, Locke's notion of property.

Brownson was both a democrat and a Democrat. During the following two years (1839-1841) he wrote a series of articles in the *Quarterly* attempting to demonstrate that the Democratic Party was fulfilling the mission of Jesus. He continued to advocate that the churches preach democracy, suggesting that the presidents and professors of educational institutions, "the Rabbis of our universities," repress their English hostility to democracy. Brownson's radical proclivity reached its zenith in "The Laboring Classes."[15] He excoriates wages as a cunning device of the devil, by which the capitalist receives all the advantages of the wage system without the expense, odium, and trouble of being a slave-holder. He is outraged at advanced nations such as England and the United States who despise the poor and abuse them shamefully, immuring them in workhouses and treating them as criminals.[16] If democracy is not to be a mere sham, a substantial equality of conditions for all must be attained. The "mights" as well as the "rights" of men should be equal. Brownson underscores again the distinction between Christ's Christianity and that of the church previously discussed in "The Kingdom of God."[17]

Singled out for special criticism in "The Laboring Classes" is marriage, the wage system, and the laws of inheritance. The work was no less than a bombshell, received by one universal scream of horror! (Brownson's own description.) He came to believe that its publication had produced a crisis in his "mental disease". The Whigs exploited it, ordering massive reprints, and distributing copies as evidence of the socialistic inclinations of the Democrats.[18] Channing and John Quincy Adams were horrified. Adams confided to his diary that this was proof that the Democratic Party was composed of Marat democrats. Emerson was delighted, Calhoun approved, though objecting to the views on inheritance. Theodore Parker published his "Thoughts on Labor," much indebted to Brownson. Francis Wayland, the president of Brown, attacked "The Laboring Classes" in his commencement address, and Whigs referred to Brownson as the American Robespierre. Brownson retorted by proposing to write a novel that would do justice to Robespierre and the French Revolution, "one of the most glorious events in human history."[19]

Brownson believed that it was necessary for the state to become truly Christian, to imbue the Democratic Party with the idea of Christian Democracy.[20] This would develop the state into an organization of mankind with the possibility of ruling the future.[21] Henry Brownson indicates that the closest approximation to his father's conception of the Church was found in the Society of Friends (Quakers). Brownson later admitted that at this point his error consisted in taking political equality with the utmost seriousness and believing that he could persuade his countrymen to adopt those measures necessary to make it a reality. He had dared to take democracy at its word and push its principles to their utmost conclusions.

However, this radical enthusiasm was stifled by the 1840 presidential elections. Harrison, the Whig, defeated Van Buren, the Democrat, by 174 electoral votes (234-60). Brownson states in *The Convert* that "the electioneering campaign of 1840... disgusted me with democracy as distinguished from constitutional republicanism, destroyed what little confidence I had in popular elections, and made me distrust both the intelligence and the instincts of the masses."[22] Moreover, it was believed by many (Brownson included) that Van Buren blamed him for the defeat. He proceeded to favor a Southern alliance to confront the dangers presented by Northern capitalism and undertook a systematic study of government as well. He began with Aristotle's *Politics*, which persuaded him that order is the necessary precondition of freedom.[23] He called for a new political party to save the Constitution and establish the reign of justice and equality, continued to correspond with Calhoun, and in "Popular Government," elaborated a theory of government similar to the Southerner's doctrine of concurrent majority.[24]

Brownson's formal education was practically nonexistent. This must have acted as a stimulant to his intellectual curiosity and voracious reading, his hyperkinetic activity, love of lengthy, noisome discussion, and confirmed his rigorous study habits. It also had a negative side. Any new work of merit, originality, or novelty had the effect of transforming him, at least for a while, into its principal authority and spokesman to the educated public, until disenchantment would set in. This occurred with Victor Cousin, whose theory of eclecticism he found especially fascinating as he believed that it reproduced the Church of the Future in a philosophic mode. Cousin was not only an eminent thinker, but a personage who had held Brownson in high regard. In Paris he told Charles Sumner that Brownson was a man of a great deal of talent, and indeed a most remarkable person; he praised him in his *Fragments Philosophiques* and indirectly recommended him for Harvard's Chair of Philosophy.[25]

Brownson reciprocated by employing Cousin's "absolute ideas" to fashion an argument for the existence of God, and, by becoming the chief exponent of the French philosopher in the U.S. published three articles, two written by himself, in 1839, on Cousin's philosophy in the *Boston Quarterly Review*. He was then invited to visit Paris and stay with the Cousin family. In a letter to Cousin (September 6, 1839) Brownson states that "your system is perfectly adapted to us because it is eminently Christian and eminently democratic.[26] By giving us the element of the supernatural (you) give us a firm basis for our faith as Christians and democrats." These plaudits were somewhat disingenuous, but surely served his purpose.[27] Three years later Brownson admitted that he had mistaken "an imbecile eclecticism" for a "powerful living synthesis."

Still a young man, Brownson had become a personage. Edgar Allen Poe referred to his logical powers in two of his tales and possibly gave a satirical portrait of him as Mr. Bullethead.[28] Channing lauded his morbidly sensitive vision on the social problems and Emerson took him to task for his incessant bluster:[29] "Brownson will never stop and listen, neither in conversation, but what is more, not in solitude."[30] He was again in the process of changing. Although he defended Transcendentalism when it came under attack, he was vexed by a series of lectures by Theodore Parker, "an enthusiast of German pedantry and *Theologische Jahrbucher*," which were later incorporated into *A Discourse of Matters Pertaining to Religion*.[31] It was a forceful apologia of the religion of humanity, a theme that was beginning to inspire repugnance in Brownson. He had become convinced that individual reason hardly sufficed. Divine guidance and grace were necessary. Brownson began to detach himself from Cousin, turning to a new arrival who was to be of enormous importance to the development of his thought—Pierre Leroux.

Looking back at his discovery of Leroux, Brownson indicates that when he read Leroux's *Réfutation de l'Éclectisme*, "it had a marvelous effect in revolutionizing my own philosophical views, or rather, of emancipating me from my subjection to the eclectic school founded by Cousin and Gouffroy."[32] He was overwhelmed by Leroux's doctrine of communion that stipulates that man lives, and only can live, in communion with that which is not himself, with his object. He lives with nature through property, with his fellow man through family and state, and with God through humanity.[33] Leroux emphasized that man cannot even think without an object. Life is jointly in the *me* and the *not-me*.

Brownson considered that the third leg of the communion-theory hobbled noticeably, tilting in the direction of pantheism. It conflates the real with the ideal that is identified with an possible able to actualize itself. Man is not progressive in himself but depends completely on the objective element that grounds him.[34] This requires communion with God on a natural and a supernatural level, but the latter was omitted by Leroux. In fact, man is constituted as a "rational existent" because of the immediate presence of God as creator, object, and light of reason, who provides him with the power to know and to love. These speculations seem to have prodded Brownson to retreat from the revolutionary romanticism that he had enthusiastically espoused. In 1842 he admitted that he had sympathized with the "Satanic School," and embraced

Cain and Lucifer as kindred spirits, believing it unmanly to kneel even before high heaven.[35]

In one of his intermittent flashes of insight, Brownson observed that the real obstacle in many minds to accepting Christianity is "want of belief in the freedom of God."[36] The freedom of God destroys that nebulous pantheism so attractive to the age and, in particular, to Leroux. It proves that God is not coterminous with nature or in bondage to it. Though Brownson discerned many flaws in Leroux's thought, he remained to some extent attached to it. He would, as an elder statesman, point to Leroux with gratitude as one of the major instruments of his conversion to Catholicism. Though banished to the outer darkness in the years following Brownson's conversion, Leroux later returned, furnished with deeper Christian roots.

While withdrawing from Cousin on the philosophical front, he was withdrawing from Channing on the religious front. Brownson wrote him a lengthy letter, really a prize essay, published later as "The Mediatorial Life of Jesus," which Emerson correctly interpreted as his repudiation of Transcendentalism.[37] Channing replied graciously if somewhat caustically: "God made you something more than to scatter random shot... though those shots may sometimes be grand ideas and may hit old errors between wind and water."[38] However, Brownson's farewell to Transcendentalism was not due to the internecine feuds that were tolerated, even welcomed, but to his growing awareness of the prime importance, the stark reality, of sin, a concept alien to the Transcendentalist mind.

Several utopian enterprises were begun under Transcendentalist inspiration. The most renowned, Brook Farm, was the brainchild of George Ripley. Several prominent members of the Club, including Emerson, Margaret Fuller, and Brownson, visited the community. Brownson's visits were anticipated with fear and trembling because of his boomingly aggressive behavior and rustic bluntness, often shouting and pounding on the table. He sent his son, Orestes Jr., to live there for a time, and published an article favoring the enterprise in the *Democratic Review* of November 1842. Isaac Hecker also visited Brook Farm and during his residence acted as community baker. However, due to the promptings of Albert Brisbane and Horace Greeley, Brook Farm was converted into a Fourierist Phalanx (community) in 1844. It continued in existence for two additional years after which it was destroyed by fire. George Ripley was left poor and discouraged.

Brook Farm formed part of a veritable explosion of utopian, usually socialistic, communities. Several were even of religious inspiration. George Rapp founded a number of communities in different states. John Humphrey Noyes founded the Oneida community near Seneca Lake, New York; Adin Ballou, the Hopedale community near Melford, Massachusetts; and the Mormons organized several groups. Nonreligious communities included Robert Owen's colony at Harmony, Ind., those inspired by Fourier and Cabet, as well as Fanny Wright's Nashoba experiment.[39] Alice Tyler estimates that more than fifty such experimental communities were set up in nineteenth century America.

In 1842 Brownson gave up the *Boston Quarterly Review* and entered into an ill-advised scheme with J. J. O'Sullivan of the *Democratic Review* to combine the two journals, with Brownson remaining a major contributor and paid on a higher scale than Hawthorne. As Father Ryan indicates, his articles were too dense, too intellectual, and when he attempted to write in a more popular vein, as in "Democracy and Liberty,"[40] he inveighed against the popular wisdom and the absolute sovereignty of an irresponsible majority.[41] There were more than five hundred cancellations. Besides writing in a highly critical way on democracy, Brownson was doing his very best to secure the presidential nomination for John C. Calhoun.

The arrangement with the *Democratic Review* was unsatisfactory to both parties and came to an end. Brownson, who it seems had forced the issue, reacted by reviving the *Boston Quarterly* under the name of *Brownson's Quarterly Review*. Its first number appeared in January 1844. After a run of over five years, its fortunes plummeted in the spring of 1849, but it was salvaged by James Sadlier and Canadian friends who also invited him to give a series of lectures at Montreal and Quebec. The association with O'Sullivan, though unfortunate, was not without fruit. The articles written for the *Democratic Review* would provide the substance of his most important political work, *The American Republic*.

Brownson was again moving in a new direction. His advocacy of Calhoun, attacks on radicalism and Fourierism, heightened religious sentiment, and chilling awareness of the ubiquity of sin, muted his passion for secular reform. He had believed that the Church of the Future would be an addenda of sorts to the Old Church. Now he began to move closer to the Old Church. During the winter of 1842-1843 he gave a series of lectures on the Middle Ages in which he condemned anti-Catholic prejudice and called for a new Catholic Church, one that would propound a universal faith for the modern world.[42] This turn was furthered by a group of essays that he wrote for *The Christian World* in which he applied Leroux's theory of communion to Christianity. He moved too rapidly. The eighth, and last, essay was not published because Brownson asserted that the Catholic Church was the living body of Christ.[43] He was satisfied as "it won the plaudits from low church to high church and even Catholic journals."

In May of 1844, Orestes Brownson called on the Roman Catholic Bishop of Boston, Msgr. Fenwick, and in June publicly announced his decision to be received into the Catholic Church.[44] The move had been prefigured in several articles published in *Brownson's Quarterly*. This was an extremely difficult, perhaps even agonizing, decision for him to make. Brownson had a poor opinion of Roman Catholics and their apologetical works, had few Catholic acquaintances, and, like most New Englanders, thought of Catholics as "ignorant, degraded, enslaved, cowardly, and imbecile."[45] The great majority of Catholics were Irish workers, who, if anything, were at the bottom of that particular barrel. He was not attracted to the Oxford Movement, Puseyism, which conceivably might have provided a convenient half-way house. He believed they were time servers. So he took the plunge: "It was, no doubt, unpleasant to take such a step, but to be eternally damned would, after all, be a great deal more unpleasanter."[46]

VI

Leroux, Newman, and Catholicity

In the period immediately preceding and following his con-version, approximately between 1842 and 1847, Brownson wrote on many themes, often perceptively, sometimes unwisely, but always vigorously. One is astonished at his surprising versatility, irked at his changes of pace, and provoked by the substance of his views, which run the gamut from tarted-up chestnuts to the novel, unexpected, and outrageous. Insofar as his views on contemporary philosophy are concerned, the two most informative pieces are an 1842 article on Pierre Leroux and his critique of a book by Hildreth, a thinker with Utilitarian views, published two years later. He was overwhelmed by the subtlety of Leroux's thought, almost to the point of discipleship. Leroux would be later criticized, amended, and exploited, but always kindly regarded. Hildreth was a minor figure who succeeded in mobilizing Brownson's scorn for Jeremy Bentham and Utilitarianism.

Leroux, Brownson indicates, is a follower of Saint-Simon, who he characterizes with customary hyperbole as "the first since Jesus to comprehend the social character of the New Testament."[1] He should be lauded for developing an embryonic social gospel and teaching moral obligation, far different from Cousin's eclecticism, which is "dumb" before the future.[2] Leroux followed Saint-Simon in using philosophical speculation to improve the conditions of mankind. Moreover, he made a major discovery, the principle of *communion*, applied it to humanity and made it the basis of a social doctrine that attempts to answer the question: "What shall I do to be saved?"

Christianity, inspired by St. Augustine, centered its attention exclusively on the improvement of the individual. Unlike Jesus, who enjoined the improvement of humanity, Christianity forgot the social dimension. Leroux's point of departure, within the wild, weltering chaos of his mind, was his belief in progress. Brownson affirms that progress is fundamentally a Christian doctrine that surfaced after eighteen hundred years of education as a clear, distinct, and scientific statement.[3] Leroux insists that to progress, man requires an *object*—that which is not himself. Progress arises from the "intershock" of the *me* and *not-me*, from communion with the other, the object. Man communes with other men and the world under three forms: family, state, and property.[4] When any of the three are organized in a way that does not admit of free development and progress, evil enters the picture. It does not proceed from any inherent depravity.

A good example is Transcendentalism, which is founded on the erroneous proposition that man can be his own object. But this cannot be; human life exists jointly in ourselves and our objects, and is generated by the intershock that occurs between the subjective and objective parts of our life. Brownson affirms that according to Leroux's thinking, philosophy demonstrates for the first time that "thy neighbor is thyself because he is thy object."[5] He believes that this generates a feeling of solidarity that can provide the basis for genuine charity yet not destroy the enlightened self-interest advocated by the (Utilitarian) philosophers. The center of Brownson's interest in Leroux is, expectedly, religious and centered on his theory of communion.

Brownson claims that Christians have only rarely understood their doctrine of Communion, the Eucharist. It was disengaged by the Church from charity to become a sacred mystery instead of a feast of love. He follows Leroux in formulating the true lesson of transubstantiation, as the solidarity of men in humanity, and of humanity, through Jesus, in God.[6] The Church, unfortunately, condemned self-love and promoted an ascetic view of the world that was foreign to the Gospels and St. Paul. This view should be reassessed to promote the reorganization of society according to the principles of the Gospel.[7]

In spite of his rather adventurous theological position, Brownson does not follow Leroux in rejecting the "old opinions" regarding heaven, hell, and individual immortality. On the contrary, he gives a surprising nod of approval to the doctrine of purgatory, considering it the adumbration of Leroux's conception of history in which "the dead still commune with us as objects to us, as we are objects to them."[8] Grounded on the premise of the universality of human solidarity, he concludes that it is impossible for any human being to attain "complete beatification" while any portion of the human race is removed from its normal condition by living a sinful life.[9] This could lead to a multiplicity of startling conclusions on both the speculative and practical levels if and when unpacked. Leroux opened many doors for Brownson. Some led to fruitful speculation, others to dead ends. Brownson believed that in this case the ladies outnumbered the tigers as Leroux's thought led him to Catholicism.

Brownson is not at his argumentative best when he is dealing with an adversary he disdains, often using him merely as an opportunity to vault to another, perhaps unrelated, topic in which he is currently interested. His article on Hildreth is a good example. He begins magisterially, declaring that any work written with the inductive method and concerning religion or morals, "will either disgust us with its nonsense, or shock us with its blasphemy."[10] However, he agrees with Hildreth's critique of the *Dial*-istic philosophers (Transcendentalists) for dishonestly purveying infidel notions in the language of faith. This has caused much confusion in the minds of good, honest people. Moreover, it leads to setting Nature up as the ultimate lawgiver, even to the point of surrendering to the license it prompts.[11] Hildreth, as a Utilitarian, makes the moral character of the act depend entirely on its generation of pleasure and pain.[12] This, notes Brownson, is a sort of demagogism carried into politics by making the conduct of the majority the standard of morality.

Changing course to discuss the education of children, he is very much the Yankee pedagogue. Surprisingly so! The child should first be taught obedience. It is the basis of respect, civility, and reverence for one's elders and superiors. Brownson believes that obedience has been ignored and the possibility of building stalwart, manly characters has gone by the board. No reasons should be given until the child is considerably advanced into maturity. To do so would destroy the foundation of respect. He concludes with a dictum which expresses the hard core of practical conservatism behind the liberal facade: "the mind, that would seek to go behind the command for its reason, is essentially impious and atheistic."[13]

One of his most noteworthy works during this period was a lengthy letter to the Rev. William Ellery Channing, later published under the title of "The Mediatorial Life of Jesus." Acknowledging his debt to Channing, Brownson credits his "Likeness to God" homily, which he compared to the Sermon on the Mount, with restoring his religious feelings. It was important for yet another reason: "I seemed suddenly to have found a father."[14] Though he was strongly opposed to psychological self-scrutiny or any form of introspection, Brownson, or his unconscious, was generous to an extreme in providing clues. The Father-theme is an unexplored mine for psychoanalytic study. The letter itself, a rejection of Channing's views, is over-determined, *i.e.*, can be interpreted in several interesting ways given Brownson's fatherless childhood.

Taking up the cudgel, Brownson goes after Channing. There is much wrong thinking concerning Jesus. Many no longer think of him as sent from God to be Redeemer and Savior but conflate God with the laws of nature. Brownson admits that both he and Channing had fallen into this error that is not only blatantly antireligious but productive of irreligion.[15] If this conflation is accepted, even those who admit that God exists virtually deny his existence by denying his freedom.[16] God's grace, not human genius or effort, provides the Mediator. Channing's position leads to the identification of the human and divine; this is the "real parent" of the deification and worship of the human soul. But if such is the grandeur of the human soul, then what need, if any, is there for a Redeemer?[17] He perceives, albeit vaguely, that the shift from theocentrism to Christocentrism leads ultimately to humanistic atheism.

Perhaps owing to a Calvinistic residue, Brownson, unlike his fellow Unitarians, Universalists, and Transcendentalists, was convinced of the flawed character of human nature. Sin will necessarily propagate itself if man is not given a new and divine life through grace. It is then a matter of ultimate concern if such a person as Jesus actually existed. He must be much more than the ethereal symbol that many, including Channing, believe him to be. To reject the person of Jesus is to reject Christianity: "the living Jesus... is the Christ and Christ is... God manifest in the flesh."[18] Brownson casts this belief in the categories provided by Leroux, which he incorporates into his own thought. To his disciples Jesus was the *object*, "the objective portion of their life by virtue of which their subjective life was developed."[19] Jesus, the Father of the New Age, makes us realize that men are not only members of one family but members of one another, linked in solidarity. This truth is expressed by the doctrine of *communion*, the word demanded by the age. By means of the communion of men with men the new life communicated by Jesus shall extend to every individual.[20]

Three years after the publication of his letter to Channing, Brownson, now a convert to Catholicism, begins to view his new faith as the key required to maintain popular liberty. He maintains that Catholicity, *viz.* the Roman Catholic Church, faith, morals and worship, is needed to preserve democratic government and secure its free, orderly and wholesome action.[21] We should not forget, Brownson urges, that our original government was not a democracy but a limited, elective aristocracy that has tended toward pure democracy since 1828. This is an unfortunate turn as "the people are fallible, both individually and collectively."[22] Because of this, if limited democracy is to be maintained and not deteriorate, it is necessary that religion exercise a degree of supervision over the people while endeavoring to foster their virtue and intelligence. The greatest danger to the United States comes from vested interests and the populist inclinations of democracy. The constitution is, to a great extent, a dead letter. The people must have a master and the only authority both above the people and free from their control is the Catholic Church.

In two substantial articles within the period of a year (July 1843-July 1844), Brownson turns his critical eye on the vicissitudes of contemporary society. He moves from observations regarding language, an enduring interest, to admonitions as a social critic. He remained convinced that language is the medium of access to reality, one whose depths remained unexplored: "we may seize the profoundest and most far-reaching truth by turning over a familiar word."[23] Words designate primitive facts. Although one may suspect that he was moving toward a position somewhere between St. Anselm and Wittgenstein, this possibility is discouraged by the examples he provides: Father Gratry, Vico and Carlyle, and his own version of overripe Emersonian purple prose.[24] Turning to the political, he makes an about-face, discarding several of the radical theories he proposed in 1836.

While again stressing the existence of wretchedness and grinding poverty within the laboring class, Brownson dismisses the "modern doctrine" of the legal right of revolution as well as the belief that violent revolution is the best way to reform society and advance humanity. Quite the opposite is true. At best, revolution is the last resort. There is no doubt that American society is in a bad way. The worship of God has been replaced by the worship of Mammon. Freedom has been contracted to the freedom of echoing the public voice, "to have no opinion of our own, and to say only what everybody believes or nobody takes the trouble to disbelieve."[25] This phenomenon, Brownson believes, is due to the effects of the expansion of education that began in the fifteenth century. Over the course of centuries, it produced a mass of half-educated men presently reflected in the composition of the American people. The greatest evil is not, as has been proposed, governmental tyranny, but lies in the industrial order and the heart of the people.[26] The division that presently exists between politics, religion and morality should be ended. This might help to curb undue optimism and correct the present inverted order of priorities.

"Come-outerism" was a phenomenon proper to the age, perhaps to any age in crisis: to escape from the existing order so as to realize a higher ideal. The flood of humanity that populated the Egyptian deserts in the early centuries of Christianity escaping from a corrupt and corrupting civilization to struggle with the forces of evil is perhaps the paradigm. It is a protest against the status quo, a pointer toward utopianism. Although Brownson admits that there may be times when the old order becomes so corrupt it needs replacing, he nevertheless insists that no man has the right to attempt its destruction on his own authority. The revolutionary spirit is at war with the religious.[27] Because of this, he believes that Come-outerism is inspired by a Satanic spirit which endeavors to destroy liberty in the name of liberty, an enterprise in which autonomy, private judgement and self-will are its favored instruments. Come-outerism ends by prostituting the mission of America, to free man from bondage.[28]

Brownson affirms that Come-outerism is the active, dominant faith of the country.[29] It entails the perversion and reversal of the proper order of things, which descend from high to low, from God to man, not from man to God. This upset is the logical outcome of two doctrines: The political doctrine that the government derives its powers from the consent of the governed, and the religious doctrine that asserts the supremacy of individual reason in matters of faith. Brownson suggests that if the Quaker doctrine of the light within is added to the preceding not only is Come-outerism legitimized but established on a divine foundation.[30]

Orestes Brownson's ambivalent relationship with John Henry Newman, to whom he has often inadvisably been compared, began with his critique of Newman's *Develop-*

ment of Christian Doctrine. As interpreted by Brownson, Newman's theory reads as follows:

> What in one age is feeling, in a succeeding age becomes opinion, and an article of faith in a still later age. This new article gives rise to a new intense feeling, which, in turn, in a subsequent age, becomes opinion, to be finally, in a later age yet, imposed as dogmatic truth.[31]

Brownson feared that if, as Newman claimed, Christianity had come into the world as a "naked and unarmed idea" and not as an institution, this would make Christianity a purely human enterprise.[32] He believed that Newman's "mother error" consisted in assuming that Christian doctrine was given originally and exclusively through the medium of the written word. He makes the point that the source of heresy is not the literal interpretation of Scripture but the attempt to deduce the faith, through private judgment, from Scripture, independently of the Church.[33]

About six months later Brownson launched a further attack on Newman and his theory of doctrinal development. He insists that the theory degrades Christianity to the level of a human heretical doctrine as it excludes the *ecclesia docens*, the teaching authority of the Church. It makes the divine passive and abandons the scholastic method for the rhetorical,[34] a charge to which Brownson must have been sensitive, especially during his tutelage by Bishop Fitzpatrick in which the scholastic method was presented as the norm. Months later he returned to the attack though in a less abrasive way (Newman was struck by his rudeness). He asserts that the theory of development rests for its logical basis on the supposition that Christian doctrine is not itself revealed truth but rather the mind's idea of it. It follows, Brownson continues, that the Church's teaching should be taken from history and philosophy.[35] Developmentalists err in overlooking the fact that the Church infallibly proposes the faith before she infallibly defines it.[36] The relations between Brownson and Newman would oscillate, on the whole remaining distant and somewhat thorny.

Though Brownson was prodded by American prelates to attack Newman, and would not otherwise have done so, his criticism was honestly framed, with perhaps a drop or two of vitriol added because of his distaste for the effete dons who comprised the Tractarian Movement. His criticism, whether or not misguided, has yet to receive an honest hearing. What he noted in Newman's work as suspect included his emphasis on the written word, the shift from the properly religious to the scholarly, from the fact to the interpretation of the fact, from a decision to a process of thought. In the Lerouxian terminology Brownson was fond of using, he noted the absence of an object. Brownson may have been mistaken about Newman but not about the course that certain High Church dons were taking. In any case, Newman himself must have had qualms, as he made a multiplicity of changes from 1845 to 1878 in the text of the essay in spite of his notorious exactitude.[37]

In "Constitutional Government," "Democracy and Liberty," and "Demagogism," Brownson studied several facets of American political life. He had a more favorable view of government than, say, Tom Paine, to whom it was a necessary evil, in spite of his views on the flawed nature of man. Government originates in the good of human nature as well as the evil.[38] Insofar as his former desire to extend democracy in the United States there are two possible options, both of which are to be rejected. The few remaining restrictions on the right of suffrage can be removed, or the constitutional checks on government action abolished. Both would serve only to exacerbate the problem. The government should be limited to matters of common concern since many of its evils proceed from favoring special interests.[39] The constitution is a necessary check on the exercise of power, which has the unfortunate tendency to exceed wholesome limits. For constitutional government to be a reality, the constitution must be protected whenever the government is disposed to violate it. This can be accomplished—with a bow to Calhoun—by the negative or veto power of the state.[40]

Brownson repeatedly mentioned his disenchantment with popular democracy on occasion of the 1840 presidential election. This led him to believe that representative government must secure guarantees other than popular suffrage or the virtue and intelligence of the people, which, in his opinion, was humbug. If the constitution, as some would have it, emanates from the people and is grounded on their will, it would be indistinguishable from no constitution at all.[41] Brownson makes it clear that democracy is an *end*, not a means, its end being the freedom and progress of all men, especially of the poorest and most numerous class.[42] He cites the commonplace division of men into stationary and movement parties, expanding it to include two groups under the latter: the radical and the conservative. The radical seeks progress by means of destruction, the conservative through and in obedience to existing institutions.[43] He counts himself among the latter.

Brownson was plagued by episodes of depression, possibly coinciding with his monumental bouts of gout, which toward the end of his life almost crystallized into a permanent disposition. This is reflected by his ongoing meditation on the decline of the United States, often followed by celebrations of the American genius and its providential role in history. He believed that the nation had declined from its primitive vigor. The stern and manly qualities of the fathers had been lost, the loss reflected in the tame and servile tone of American literature. This descent is at least partly due to the habit of catering to the masses, seeking to echo popular opinion, not to correct and mold it. He views this as the direct result of the principle of responsibility to the people embraced by the politicians.[44] With distressing prescience, Brownson sees the day of the demagogue fast approaching: "our liberties, and the whole action of the government will be at the mercy of the sly, cunning, adroit, intriguing, selfish demagogues, whom our country... has a direct and strong tendency to multiply."[45]

Brownson is moving away from radicalism and revolutionary fervor toward a centrist position which evidences both conservative and liberal motives, yet he still harbors a radical substratum. There is a move toward a more objective position, perhaps stimulated by Leroux. The cult of progress, albeit modified, was retained as the centerpiece of his thought. He also retains and to some extent rethinks much of the Old Theology, while continuing to accuse Christianity of having perverted the pristine Christianity preached by Jesus. Once he reaffirms the reality and centrality of the person of Jesus Christ, these attacks begin to diminish. Catholicity becomes the watchword, the true religion, and the key which fits the lock of democracy, guaranteeing popular liberty while curbing its anarchic inclinations.

While still sympathizing with the poor and disadvantaged, Brownson rejects the legal right of revolution. The Newman affair sets the tone of his future relations with the Oxford Movement as well as his often unfortunate interventions in Catholic intramural struggles. Several of the prelates view him and use him as conversation piece, trophy, adviser, and

hired gun. Brownson, now an orthodox Roman Catholic, is
moving in the direction of a fuller, complete understanding of
his new faith, and of a more accurate appraisal of its practical workings. He makes an earnest attempt to integrate his
new-found Catholicism with his prior views on social justice,
the role of Christianity, progress, liberalism, and with the not
negligible residue of his utopianism.

VII

Introibo

Orestes Augustus Brownson was forty-one years of age when he was received into the Catholic Church on October 20, 1844, about a year before the reception of John Henry Newman. His efforts to persuade friends and adherents to follow his path to Rome produced a meager harvest: some friends and his family, with son Orestes, Jr., bringing up the rear. Bishop Fenwick, a Jesuit and a Marylander, charmed and edified him: "an excellent man, learned, polite, easy, affable, affectionate, and exceedingly warm hearted."[1] The coadjutor bishop, John B. Fitzpatrick, Boston-born and educated by the Sulpicians at Paris, was designated as his instructor. He was a markedly different personality from Bishop Fenwick and from Brownson. Perhaps an unfortunate choice. Opinions differ. Though Brownson would later praise him fulsomely, they seem to have gotten along fitfully. Isaac Hecker referred to Fitzpatrick as "the hierarchical exponent of all that was traditional and commonplace in Catholic public life,"[2] and he, as a near-disciple and close friend of Brownson, would be in a position to know. Nevertheless, his opinion should be accepted with caution as Hecker tended to make judgments through the prism of his current enthusiasm.

Perhaps Fitzpatrick was cowed by Brownson's fame and intellectual attainments or irked by his habits of independence and frank dislike for many things Catholic. In any case, Brownson began to study Catholic theology, attempted meditation according to the method of St. Ignatius' *Spiritual Exercises* with indifferent success, and engaged in pious devotions such as wearing a scapular and reciting the rosary. Later, Isaac Hecker—now Father Hecker—sent him a copy of Gorres' *Die Christliche Mystik,* together with a discipline (a small whip) and threatened to send hair-shirts.[3] Brownson was not addicted to corporeal penance. It is doubtful if the discipline was used, at least on a regular basis. His conversion did spark his appetite. After two years his once gaunt frame tipped the scales at 250 lbs. He found that Catholics were better than he had anticipated, which was very little indeed. He still found that many Catholics had unattractive, even repulsive, traits: "In our cities may be found... a comparatively numerous population, nominally Catholic, who are no credit to their religion, to the land of their birth, or to that of their adoption... children... to become recruits to our vicious population, our rowdies, and our criminals."[4]

Bishop Fitzpatrick was a hard taskmaster. All of Brownson's articles concerning theology were sent to him for censorship. He was dissuaded from continuing to advocate Leroux's theory of communion, and was obliged to change his method and style to the point that some readers became unsettled, several writing to voice their dismay.[5] For about five years Brownson discussed philosophical and theological matters in borrowed and ill-fitting garb, oddly conventional and scholastic, within an alien universe of discourse. Much of the old Brownson remained, however. Fitzpatrick may have muted his spontaneity but not his character nor his inclination to use a battle ax to crush a butterfly.

The Catholic bishops were not reluctant to employ the services of their prize convert. Brownson was at the height of his fame and a neophyte to the serpentine ways of clerical politics. In 1846 Bishop Fitzpatrick (now Bishop of Boston), prodded by Archbishop Purcell of Cincinnati, persuaded Brownson to attack John Henry Newman's *Essay on the Development of Christian Doctrine*, possibly emulating the tactic of the Middle Kingdom of using one barbarian to check another barbarian. Six years later, Brownson castigated John Brande Morris, an Oxford convert, accusing the Tractarians of intellectual dishonesty and scored Newman's "narrow views."[6] Brownson simply did not believe that certainty could be obtained from accumulated possibilities nor that any substantial development had actually taken place in Catholic doctrine. He believed that these men had come to Catholicism because of aesthetic and intellectual reasons, not properly religious ones. Their insular arrogance galled him as much as did the clannishness of the Irish. Sir John Acton, in his *American Diaries*, reports a conversation with Brownson at his house at Chelsea: "Brownson is very sorry about the hostility he has produced, but quite convinced of Newman's errors, though of course he admits developments of another kind."[7]

Brownson continued to turn more conservative. One of his articles was rejected by the *American Whig Review* because it was considered rabidly anti-democratic. The year of revolution (1848) witnessed a more pronounced turn to the right. He attacked Lammenais, whom he had previously admired greatly. What he had previously stated as the authentic creed of Jesus and which was summarized (1842) by the motto "Union and Progress," was substantially modified. He scored the "heresy" that originated in the attempt to adapt the Church to dominant ideas and sentiment. Socialism, the premier ideology, was no more than Protestantism gone to seed, "pantheism adopted to the apprehensions of the vulgar."[8] He went as far as to protest against the official welcome given Kossuth, the Hungarian revolutionary, and to attack the Catholic press as he held it, with the secular press, responsible for the low moral tone of the public and its religious indifference. Ineluctably, the press brought literature down to "the tastes and attainments of the unreasoning, undisciplined, and conceited multitude."[9]

When *Brownson's Quarterly Review* suffered from economic troubles, he was aided not only by his Canadian friends, but by the American Catholic bishops, who issued a statement of support that was placed on the cover of every issue. The *Review* burgeoned, and by 1853 enjoyed a higher circulation than in 1845.[10] When he began to put Transcendentalism under the gun, Brownson was in turn attacked by some of his former associates. Theodore Parker spoke of Brownson as "intellectual always, but spiritual never... not a Christian, but only a verbal index of Christianity,"[11] probably an exaggeration but not without a foundation in reality. To aggravate the situation, Brownson began to emphasize the dogma of *Extra Ecclesiam nulla salus*, interpreting it with the utmost strictness. He believed it should be preached in all its rigor so as to head off the rising tide of latitudinarianism. Otherwise, any argument that stressed the necessity of professing Christianity for salvation "will have no more effect on them than rain on a duck's back."[12]

Off on another tangent, Brownson was persuaded by his reading of de Maistre to think of the Constitution as the living soul of the nation, a sort of distillate of the habits, traditions, customs, and manners of a people. The Constitution is that by which a nation is constituted as a nation and empowered to establish a national life. However, as a firm republican, his interpretation differed from that of the monarchist de Maistre. Acton reported to his mentor Dollinger that Brownson set Burke and de Maistre above all other political writers.[13] This was quite a reversal for a man who had once castigated Burke for his vigorous opposition to the French Revolution. He would later, during the liberal interim of 1860-1864, recover his predilection for Lammenais, Montalembert, and other thinkers of the liberal wing of French Catholicism.

Bishop Fitzpatrick was prone to leave Brownson hanging. The slanderous "The Atheism of Brownson's Review" was simply ignored by the bishop.[14] However, it should be pointed out that this lack of support, though it must have affected Brownson adversely, does not appear to have strained their relationship to the breaking point, as was later the case with Archbishop Hughes of New York. When Fitzpatrick visited Europe in 1854, Brownson ceased to submit his articles for censorship. He detached himself from a subordination that he must have considered, at best, distasteful; but the Bishop brought with him a commendation from Pope Pius IX, which must have soothed whatever chagrin he harbored. The ambivalence of their relationship makes it difficult to ascertain those particulars that make conjecture a rewarding enterprise.

Brownson was a Yankee, proud of his English heritage, a recent Transcendentalist associate, and somewhat ill at ease in his new surroundings. He was in an awkward position to become the champion of Irish Catholic immigrants but circumstance forced him into the role. He became a casualty of the Nativist controversy. Like John Adams before him, Brownson defended the people while emphasizing their inferiority, a sure recipe for unpopularity. The statistics were ominous. In 1830 only four hundred thousand out of a population

of thirteen million, were foreign-born. Within the next twenty
years, almost two and a half million immigrants flooded the
country. The popular jibe was that the nation England governed, governed America. The situation was not helped by the
belief among the supporters of Henry Clay that the Irish immigrant vote was responsible for his defeat in 1844.[15]

Native-born Americans began to form associations to
combat the influence, real or imagined, of the immigrants,
with the Irish Catholics as their prime targets. Serious inci-
dents occurred. In Charleston, a convent was burned (1834)
and the Irish sections of Boston and Philadelphia were looted.
At the time Brownson was under instruction at Boston, a
threeday riot took place in Philadelphia. Cannon were fired,
several churches were destroyed, and sixty-three persons
killed or wounded.[16] The situation had become hazardous,
not unlike the immigrant invasion and popular reactions of
the present day. The immigrants, standing by their rights,
were attempting to put down roots in a new land. The native-
born, fearful that their way of life was endangered and that
an undesirable metamorphosis was threatening the nation,
reacted violently.

Brownson eventually became unpopular with both
Nativists and Irish Catholics. The former he further alienated
by his polemical writings, as they were strident, aggressive,
making claims in favor of Papal supremacy, claims that were,
not unreasonably, interpreted as disloyalty to the United
States. The fear grew, shared by Brownson to some degree,
that the American Catholic Church was a Celtic institution
and would be unable to become authentically American.
Moreover, Brownson insisted on the real existence of an
American nationality predominantly of English origin and
descent and believed that this spirit should ultimately orient
and structure the other nationalities that would arrive on

American shores. The nation had a natural right to preserve itself and everything that constituted it and to guard against foreign corruption.

He was also convinced that Catholicity was essential for the preservation of authentic democratic government; vivified by Catholicity, democracy might become the best form of government. Otherwise, democracy was in danger of falling victim to its intrinsic weaknesses and becoming the worst form, "as our own experience... will soon demonstrate."[17] He notes that a division of Americans is already taking place and distinguishes between Old America, the genuine America that adheres to constitutional republicanism, and New America, the bastard America, radical, ultra-democratic, and revolutionary.[18] These notions, added to his view that naturalization is not a right but a privilege, made him almost as unpopular with the majority of the immigrant group as he was with the Nativists. He literally floored a man who called him a traitor for converting to Catholicism.

Apart from his often derogatory comments regarding the Irish immigrant class and their dangerous proclivities, Brownson retained sympathy for key democratic tenets. He did not want the pendulum to swing backwards and create the impression among Catholics that the only choice left to them was between the Church and Caesarism on the one hand, and liberty and infidelity on the other. Every effort should be made to disconnect religion from the cause of despotism.[19] Brownson was also reevaluating his views on radical democracy. In an article published in 1851, he made the point that the members of the 1787 Convention

> did not see that the Social Contract was already in Locke's *Essay on Government*, and that the French Revolution and all its horrors were in the Social

Contact, and that all the modern red-republicanism, socialism, and communism were in the French
Revolution. They had no suspicion of the poison
contained in the phrase 'sovereignty of the people'—a phrase in their sense so innocent and so
just.[20]

He was wary of the Catholic immigrant reverence for
authority, believing that it made the Irish distrust the independence and personal dignity of the American, his disposition to bow to laws and not to persons. Many believed that
the American was a rebel by instinct and, if not an unbeliever,
was certainly at odds with the obedience required by the
Gospel. Nevertheless, he did admire the Irish lack of respect
for the mob, mere wealth, and public opinion, qualities
uncommon among Americans. He hoped that the immigrants
would, within a few years, become, as he put it, "the Americans of Americans" as on them will rest the "glorious work"
of preserving American civilization and "realizing the hopes
of our great and growing Republic."[21] Brownson wavered
between fear of European despotism and fear of radical
democracy, slowly coming to believe, with intermittent periods of doubt, that the latter was the greater danger both to
Catholicism and the American Republic.

Though his defense of the Catholic immigrant was both
vigorous and reasonable, as was his attack on the Know-
Nothings of Nativism,[22] Brownson offended the Irish immigrant as well as highly placed bishops such as Hughes,
Purcell, and O'Connor. Schlesinger relates that in July and
August 1854, he was censured in at least nine Catholic journals for insulting honest men and kindling anti-Irish feelings.[23] These contretemps must have been hard to take,
especially after entering the lists in favor of a group he did not

much like or admire. The section of the American hierarchy that he managed to alienate gave him little rest until his death. The uproar caused by the Nativist controversy reached the point that Archbishop Kenrick of Baltimore asked Brownson to remove the Bishop's 1844 letter of endorsement from the cover of *Brownson's Quarterly*. He was put in a corner, attempting to defend his right to be a Catholic against Americans, and his right to be an American against Catholics.

At this time, Brownson reviewed Father Hecker's *Questions of the Soul*. Gilhooley indicates that this marks the full return of the American Dream: to realize the idea of a Christian society.[24] This is so, but the praise accorded *Questions of the Soul* should be balanced by the criticisms launched at *Aspirations of Nature*. The claims of friendship inclined Brownson to a leniency for which future retribution would often be the price. However, Brownson praises *Questions* as a remarkable book, one of the few genuine American books our country can boast. He praises the author's devotion to truth, earnestness of spirit, and longing after perfection.[25] Moreover, Brownson affirms that the special mission of the United States is "the sublime work of realizing the idea of Christian society, and of setting the example of a truly great, noble, Catholic people."[26] This theme would often be repeated in the future.

However, in his review of *Aspirations* he takes Father Hecker to task for supposing that reason and nature aspire to supernatural beatitude. They do not. They cannot rise above nature. Brownson insists that Hecker's view was not only theologically mistaken, based on an erroneous notion of the gravity of original sin, but practically counterproductive: "once you concede to non-Catholics that they already hold our first principles, they will rest satisfied with themselves and not convert."[27] This would be the crux of their disagreements from this point on.

Brownson continued to harass the Abolitionists. He denounced the Mexican War as an unjustified adventure and the anti-Spanish filibusterism in Cuba that culminated in the attempted incursions of 1850 and 1851 and the execution of Col. Crittenden and his men. Writing to the Spanish ambassador, he has harsh words for Americans: "we are vain boasters, and boast always of the virtues we lack.... Let us... endeavor to see ourselves for once as we really are."[28] In turn, the ambassador's wife, Fanny Calderon de la Barca, referred to Brownson as the Balmes of America. A signal honor now came from an unexpected source. John Henry Newman, who had recently been appointed Rector of the proposed Catholic University in Ireland, invited Brownson to give a series of lectures during 1854-1855. The Catholic intellectual elite were invited, including Professor Dollinger of later Modernist fame. The subject Brownson would teach was geography, which may have been a convenient label for everything and nothing. Could it have been a fine thrust of sarcasm from a victim of Brownson's invective?

Brownson demurred. Acton then wrote urging him to come and lecture on whatever he pleased, "the vast field of philosophy will be yours." Moreover, he was encouraged to found a "Catholic school" of thought and arm it with the principles of sound philosophy.[29] Newman wrote in the same vein. Brownson now accepted, but the Nativist controversy and its sequelae had already sent ripples across the Atlantic. Newman suggested an indefinite postponement and Brownson withdrew his acceptance in a letter of Sept. 12, 1854. Newman was later to write, in the postscript of a letter to Hope Scott: "old Brownson's coming is suspended. He has been treading on the toes of the great Irish nation."[30] Ironically, Newman also fell victim to the prelates. His bishopric *in partibus,* which was under consideration, was effectively blocked.

At home, Brownson suspected Bishop Purcell as the principal instigator. He began to have kinder feelings toward Newman, even praising him in reviewing *Loss and Gain.* But his animadversion to the Tractarians perdured and, years later, he dismissed Newman's letter to the Duke of Norfolk as wishy-washy. Newman was also irked. He told a friend in 1857: "I am opposed to laymen writing theology on the same principle as I am against amateur doctors... for this reason I am disgusted with Brownson."[31] Brownson had a different temperament from the genteel, donnish Newman and believed that the velvet glove approach was counterproductive. Contemporary heretics did not doubt the ability or the learning of Catholics but rather their sincerity. The truth should be stated bluntly and baldly. Happily, this tactic managed to coincide with his own inclinations. Maynard put it nicely when he stated that Brownson thought that a man could not be telling the truth unless he bellowed it; this trait caused more damage than he realized.[32] He would often startle his friends and associates with his explosive behavior. This alone distanced him, at least temperamentally, from the ultra-refined Newman. They were opposites, perhaps even caricatures of their respective species.

He did not begin his study of Augustine, Aquinas, and other medieval and Catholic thinkers until he was in his early forties, obliged by circumstance to merge these authors with prior gleanings, new enthusiasms, and his own efforts at synthesis. He took issue with St. Thomas Aquinas on the question of universals, following William of Champeaux's moderate realism; on the Agent Intellect, which he identified with Augustine's inner teacher; and on the notion of Being, which he considered, like Duns Scotus, a univocal, not an

analogous term.[33] Among arguments attempting to prove
God's existence, Brownson favors the *a priori* arguments such
as Anselm's *Proslogion*, elaborating his own variations,[34]
while leaning away from *a posteriori* arguments such as St.
Thomas' *quinque viae*. Father Bertin Farrell, though he can
be faulted for glaring misconceptions, does succeed in showing that Brownson's thought on God is not Thomistic.[35]

Perhaps to complement these abstruse speculations,
Brownson, in 1854, wrote a rather odd book, *The Spirit-
Rapper*. Using an autobiographical form, he investigates the
phenomenon of spiritism. The theme was very much in the air.
He perceived it not only as a congeries of isolated phenomena
but an agenda revealing the presence of satanic forces and purposes. Maynard perhaps exaggerates when he views it as
Brownson's attempt to explain history in terms of the conflict
between God and Satan,[36] a sort of *De Civitate Dei* in minia-
ture. Brownson was probably simply attempting to show how
the superstitions of the age, the prevailing moral unsettlement,
and the radical ethos of revolutionary democracy energized
each other by intertwining, receiving their inspiration and
strength from subterranean powers. Here again he was pre-
scient as the increasing presence of the occult within Christianity in the twentieth century clearly demonstrates.

Meanwhile, he was again at work antagonizing the clergy
by launching an attack on the Gallicanism of the American
Church, drawing fire from influential prelates such as Archbishop Hughes—who considered it inopportune—Bishop
O'Connor, and Archbishop Purcell, who had advised Brownson to launch the attack in the first place.[37] Catholic editors
such as Huntington, McMaster, and Henry Major joined in
the barrage, as did his fiercest critic, the Protestant Fenian,
John Mitchell, editor of the *Citizen*, who blasted him royally:

You, Doctor Orestes, you more than any one living man, have aroused and kindled this strong anti-Catholic, and therefore anti-Irish spirit in America, by your ultra-Catholic and antirepublican teachings and writings.[38]

Dr. Orestes was supported by the Bishops Kenrick and Miege (St. Louis & Baltimore). Acton, in a letter to Dollinger, called him an eager Papalist under the thumb of Bishop Fitzpatrick.[39]

Hughes would later point out that Brownson's conversion was turning into a mixed blessing. As Van Wyck Brooks wrote to Maynard, Brownson "was an intellectual dynamo running in a void," adding that "I don't believe that at the time the American Catholic public either needed or knew how to use the kind of mind he brought them."[40] This is not far off the mark. The situation possibly was doubly agonizing for Brownson as he must have felt both ill-used and misunderstood. He viewed the Catholic intellectual scene in the United States with frank distaste, as the lowest link on a chain of inverse evolution. Nevertheless, it must be admitted that he was also to blame. His inept maneuverings, oscillations, character flaws, and lack of candor caused by his glorified self-image, helped not at all.

Part of his difficulty and much of his disenchantment with Catholics and the clergy arose from a naivete concerning the workings of the American Catholic Church. The often exaggerated distance between the clergy and their flock often generated attitudes not only of obedience but of servility, as did the gap between prelate and priest, both variations on the theme of the psychology of minor differences which makes for rough sailing. At its worst, it can produce an upside-down world structured by custom and rote. But even at its best, it produces changes of pace and minor defects that become glaringly evident to a neophyte such as Orestes Brownson.

The Nativist controversy and its attendant difficulties, perhaps the relation with Bishop Fitzpatrick, and a number of other factors of a personal, vocational, and familial nature had made Boston inhospitable. On August 25, 1855, Brownson wrote Hecker complaining that the diocese had become more and more Irish and that he would like "to remove to your city." Father Hecker, always ready to be of help, spoke to Archbishop Hughes, and was told that Brownson would be most welcome in his archdiocese. In the fall of 1855 Brownson packed up his family and his *Quarterly Review* and moved to New York. Unfortunately, his difficulties were only beginning.

VIII

They are Legion

Socialism and its relation to Catholicity occupy much of Brownson's interest in the period of about seven years from 1848 to 1855. This interest extends to Protestantism, which Brownson believed was socialism's original point of departure. Not unlike the views of the Spanish thinker Donoso Cortes,[1] he contends that Protestantism is the major premise, which, when unpacked logically, leads to socialism as one of its conclusions. He was aware that socialism exercises a prodigious influence on the unconscious level as well as on the conscious, "in one form or another... [it]... has already taken possession of the age" and is armed for battle.[2] Even those who reject socialism accept those very principles of which it is the invincible development. These principles are ubiquitous: "there is an invincible logic in society which pushes it to the realization of the last consequences of its principles."[3] Socialism is the last surge of the Protestant Reformation.

Brownson's view of Protestantism was negative, combative, and idiosyncratic. He agreed with its partisans that it represented an uprising in favor of liberty, but added that it was the liberty of the world, the flesh, and the devil. He did not think that Protestantism was an authentic religion, its Catholic residue excepted, but rather a political and social movement on behalf of the secular order. Because of this, Protestantism should be considered primarily as a revolt of the flesh against God, not as a false theology.[4] Catholicity is the only safe port. As Brownson stated in his encomium of Bishop Fenwick, were salvation to be attainable out of the Catholic Church, there would be no solid reason for joining her.[5] As he grew older, Brownson became even more vituperative, lashing out at Presbyterians, Anglicans, and Methodists: Satan was the first Protestant.[6]

The only solution to the revolutionary ideology and the upset that threaten society is to recall humanity to sound first principles. He had become the victim of his own relentless logic when, in "The Laboring Classes," he reasoned that if political equality is a good, then social equality is also a good. But he came to realize that social equality leads necessarily to the annihilation of religion, government, property, and family.[7] Once the socialist premises are granted, the conclusions follow necessarily. It follows that these premises must be reexamined and their underlying principles rejected. This is a doubly difficult task when socialism is presented under a Christian facade and couched in the language of the Gospel. Channing in the United States and Lammenais in France are prime examples.

Brownson had previously advocated, and would in the future again advocate, that Christianity form an alliance with the forces of liberty, so as to correct prevalent abuses.[8] But at present and after his liberal hiatus of 1860-1864, he considered this attitude mistaken and a dangerous lure to Catholics. Socialists employ texts from Scripture and with perverse ingenuity, denounce Christianity in the name of Christianity, and defy God in the name of God. They use Christian symbols, but change their traditional meaning to one in tune with their ideology. As Brownson acutely observes, this eviscerates *democracy excluded*

Catholicity of its memory and clears the field for the constitution of a "counterfeit Catholicity."[9]

The Catholic Church is bound to no particular form of government or social organization, nor should it be. Its mandate to seek good and avoid evil does not require participation in revolutionary movements. However, the principle of these movements, exclusive democracy, is often proposed as the only acceptable form of government. This, Brownson insists, cannot be accepted by the Church as it would bind her to democracy. It would, in effect, erect democracy into a dogma of faith.[10] He suggests that if this were the case, missionaries in countries where democracy does not exist would be conscience-bound to revolutionize the state. The Church would play into the hands of enraged populations who, lusting after earthly goods, are hardly the friends of religious freedom.[11] Whether or not this is an adumbration of liberation theology and its anticipatory rejection, it is nevertheless a tribute to his acuity.

Brownson, in an interesting turn, places Pierre Leroux head to head with Donoso Cortés. With customary hyperbole he says they are the authors of the two most profound works to be found in the entire range of modern political literature. Donoso's is written from the perspective of Catholicity, Leroux's from the viewpoint of pantheistic humanitarianism.[12] Though he credits Donoso with a higher order of genius, he is obviously more interested in Leroux, the representative of that which is positive in socialism. However, he does mark a theory of Donoso's as worthy of praise: the view that human society originates and finds its prototype in the divine society of the Holy Trinity, which is the radiant center of the principle of Unity and Diversity, the touchstone of created reality.[13] After this nod to Donoso, he passes on to Leroux.

Philanthropy was one of the bugbears Brownson constantly savages. In this article, "Liberalism and Socialism," he takes a different tack, indicating that it is the only form that the purest and best in religion can assume outside the Christian Church. Philanthropy is, however, a weak substitute and acts as the purveyor of both liberalism and socialism. The Church has the task of placing obstacles in the way of these developments. It should complement the state by teaching morals and defining right. The task of the state is to impose the determinations presented to it by the Church.[14] State and Church complement each other as power complements authority. The State appeals to the authority of the Church, and when the Church makes its determinations, the State uses its power to enforce them.

Turning to Leroux's theory of communion, he asserts that it must be accepted by the Christian although it is incomplete and can find its fulfillment only within the Catholic Church.[15] While reviewing the theory, Brownson modifies the notion of solidarity, noting that solidarity is a temporal, as well as a spatial, phenomenon, that it embraces all men in all ages, and links, in indissoluble life, the first man and the last.[16] Studying Leroux's speculations from a Catholic perspective, he finds that his error consists in his assumption that Catholic dogmas symbolize natural truths, as instanced by his doctrine of communion. But the reverse is true. The human symbolizes, expresses, the divine. Natural truths symbolize dogmas.[17] But, on the whole, Leroux is right. Man has a threefold nature and lives by communion with God (in religion), man (in society), and nature (in property); whatever interferes with this threefold communion is repugnant to God and noxious to humanity. Brownson ends with some highly significant words: "what we aimed at before our conversion is still dear to us, and we are still, in some sense, a man of our age."[18] This can be interpreted as a hint, made in 1855, of the coming turn toward liberalism that would take place in 1860-1864.

Two years previously, Brownson had commented on a letter of Donoso Cortés to *El Heraldo* of Madrid in which he stigmatized the expression "human right" as "*viciosa*" [vicious]. This had been taken up by the editor of *Civilità Cattolica* and characterized as hyperbolical and exaggerated.[19] Brownson knew that to Donoso all rights are, strictly speaking, God's rights. Consequently man only has duties *vis-à-vis* God, as God was the immediate ground of man's obligation to conform to the order of nature. Donoso's opponents believed that God was the mediate ground of this obligation and based the right of government and duty of the subject on social necessity. Brownson anathematized this view as political atheism, as it effects the divorce of politics from religion. This is, he indicates, a characteristic error of the age, the "gangrene" of modern society.[20] He veers from Donoso's position in affirming that man does enjoy real, though not autonomous, rights transferred to us by God's will.[21]

The lengthiest, though hardly the most important, work during this period was his last effort at autobiography, *The Spirit-Rapper* (1854). Though decidedly bizarre, it can be considered as a tribute to his versatility... or credulity. Here, Brownson attempts to establish a connection between spiritism, and its exotic manifestations such as mesmerism and clairvoyance, with radicalism, socialism, and philanthropy. He maintained that spiritism was the facade covering revolutionary ideology, attractive to Anglo-Americans because of their love of novelty, fascination with the bizarre, and constitutional hyperkineticism, always craving novel stimuli.[22] The protagonist moves through a surrealistic landscape populated by the more outlandish denizens of his age, a company very similar to that described by Emerson at a meeting of the Friends of Universal Reform. They consider themselves a combination of abolitionist, philanthropist, and world-reformer, and expectantly await the dawning of a new age in which the female gender would predominate.[23] They were persuaded that humanity would soon be able to avail itself of the hidden powers of nature to become gods and enjoy every conceivable good summarized in the word "liberty."[24]

This motley group is represented in *The Spirit-Rapper* by three characters: Mr. Edgerton, a fanciful caricature of Emerson, given to speculation, dietetic reform, and musings on the bubbleosity of the bubble; Miss Rose Winters, a zealous opponent of Biblical authority; and Signor Giovanni Urbini, a partisan of radical democracy who advocates "the people-king, the people-pontiff, the people-god."[25] Together they represent the Spirit of the Age, which is peremptorily demanding a new order of things.[26] The protagonist's "scientific experiments" add a further dimension to the plot as he is persuaded that he is about to discover an invisible, elemental, impersonal force, which would contribute to the advancement of their goals. At the dark center of this enterprise Brownson recognizes Satan unbound.

Among much that is pedestrian, graceless, even credulous, Brownson touches on a theme that will be found later: that the demonic strategy to topple Christianity consists in surreptitiously introducing another religion from within, a caricature or malevolent double in harmony with the flesh and the spirit of the age.[27] This scheme will be put into effect while proclaiming that its goal is merely to divorce religion from politics and to democratize the Church. This Christian double will be made especially attractive by the sentimental, philanthropic character it assumes, and it will be made respectable by covering it with the umbrella of progress.[28] As late as June 1869, he is warning of the dangers posed by the astonishing surge of spiritism that has taken place since 1847: "He (Satan) has done wonders in our day as philanthropist, and met with marvelous success as a humanitarian, and will, perhaps, meet with more still as the champion of free love and women's rights."[29]

Heathenism presents a further danger. It stems, as with all negativities, from original sin, which fractured the hierarchical order by which the body was subjected to the soul. This fracture also affects the political order. As a result the secular realm renounced its subordination to the spiritual.[30] Brownson faults the Renaissance for effecting this upset, for by emancipating the secular from the spiritual it "left men to their corrupt nature, the inexhaustible fountain of all heathenism."[31] Heathenism neglects grace to follow its own compulsion, placing the secular above the spiritual and the creature above the Creator. Heresy is merely inchoate heathenism that requires only time and freedom to fully develop.

Brownson firmly believed that the present era aspires to reproduce the heathen order. This attitude is exemplified by the Transcendentalist dictum of "acting out ourselves," reinforced by the "whimpering sentimentality characteristic of our times."[32] Nevertheless, in spite of its many objections, the first duty of civil government is to protect the Church and safeguard freedom of religion. In an unusual but intriguing burst of prognostication, Brownson states that Russia and America, "the two aggressive powers of the age... threaten to meet in China or India, and, on the plains of that old Asiatic continent, to dispute the empire of the world."[33] However, the triumph of either will signify the triumph of heathenism and the oppression of the Church. This surprising prediction loses something of its force when Brownson chooses Austria (!) as the possible leader of the resistance to the two behemoths.[34]

This may be interpreted as a diminished version of St. Augustine's awesome scenario in which two cities or pyramids of loyalty engage in a monumental struggle that lasts as long as does history: Catholicity and Heathenism at war, with heathenism triumphant on the natural level and Catholicity on the supernatural, ushering in the world-to-come. This interpretation is attractive and not beyond the bounds of feasibility, but it fails to deal with Brownson's narrow conception of time, in which history is contracted to provide a basis for prediction, with the two cities identified with Church and anti-Church. Though this takes something away from Augustine's grandiose conception, it undoubtedly dances to Brownson's piper.

The exterior face of Brownson's thought is often in contradiction to his subliminal thoughts and attitudes, which he loudly professed to be of no importance. The unconscious tends to peek through and even emerges on the conscious level to mold the patterns of his thought. In spite of his violent attacks on liberalism and socialism, there linger residues of sympathy—anchored in the deeper regions of the soul—which would surface intermittently. A clear adumbration of his forthcoming turn toward liberalism is found in his 1856 article, "Protestants in the Sixteenth Century":

> Our great study... should now be, both in this country and in Europe, to *avoid* binding ourselves to an order of things that has passed or is passing away, and to prepare ourselves for the future which is advancing. We must accept both for the sake of religion and of society, the *new order*, as it comes up and establishes itself.[35]

Though he continued to oppose the principles of the revolutionary movements of 1848, he was convinced that the democratic transformation of Christendom would finally be effected. It was necessary to prepare for its success as "the revolution, in some form, will go on."[36] Today, the Catholic Church, perhaps beginning with the pontificate of Pope John XXIII, reflects this belief to some extent.

This is a turnabout! Brownson the Weathercock! Eight years previously he had severely criticized the view that the Church should abandon the governments and appeal to the people, forming an alliance between religion and liberty.[37] At the time he stated that this would compromise the divine mission of the Church, and propose a particular form of government—democracy—as an article of faith,[38] both of which are unacceptable. Brownson's wavering on a point of such importance is difficult to understand. Was he a closet liberal awaiting liberation? A conservative with episodes of unsettlement? Or perhaps a fragile personality at the mercy of personal, financial, or political considerations that prodded him serendipitously in different directions? A man of enormous ego guided by his love of the public spotlight and his position as reigning Catholic guru? Or perhaps simply a clear and penetrating mind, moving in synchronization with the objective factors at work in history?

Slavery was an endemic problem to the American nation. It was both political and religious. In 1851 Brownson, who had previously condemned slavery as immoral, proposed that it was not a *malum in se*, an evil in itself. If the master has not participated in the slave trade, treats his slaves with humanity, and diligently watches over their moral and religious well-being, he cannot be condemned.[39] It is permitted by U.S. law, since the Constitution recognizes slaves as property. To this he added emotional considerations which Brownson shared with the white majority. Even the freed Negro was not spared:

> They are the pests of our Northern cities, especially since they have come under the protection of the philanthropists... with few honorable exceptions, they are low and degraded, steeped in vice and overflowing with crime.[40]

Envisaging with horror the prospect of two or three million slaves being given freedom and the right to vote, Brownson exclaims that "the whole country would be at the mercy of the lowest and most worthless of our demagogues."[41]

William Seward had argued in favor of abolition from the point of view of the "higher law." Brownson agreed that such a law existed. It is the law of God and is situated on a level even higher than the Constitution. Nevertheless, he considers that Seward does not have the right, while holding a seat in the Senate under the Constitution, to appeal to a higher law, because in doing so, he denies the very authority by which he holds his seat.[42] However, Brownson continues to deplore slavery. In July of 1851, he indicates that if slavery did not already exist in the United States, he would oppose it by all lawful means.[43] It is a moral wrong. However, as it is impossible to make this world a paradise or its inhabitants saints, we are obliged to tolerate it. It is interesting to note that this is fundamentally the same argument used by several of the schoolmen, including Aquinas, to justify prostitution.[44]

By law slaves are property. Therefore, to attack slavery is, in principle, to attack private property and open the gates to tyranny by the state. Brownson has no use for the Abolitionists, "free-soil fanatics," who he excoriates as wild radicals, men for whom it is not enough to sin from passion or appetite but who sin from principle in their "zeal for reversing." This propensity, left to its own devices, would go as far as to change the natural relation of the sexes.[45] Brownson was very much aware that slavery was of enormous political importance, one of the main cards to be played in the power game between Northern and Southern interests. The moral canopy that covered it served only to disguise these moves and countermoves. The conflict would explode into internecine warfare in the period of about a decade.

Native Americanism was a more immediate problem. Brownson's life can be understood as a long exercise in irony. In spite of his negative views concerning Negroes, he was one of the few Catholics to favor emancipation. In spite of his jaundiced opinion of the Irish immigrants, he was one of their most prominent defenders. In both cases, the religious and moral imperatives won the day against his Yankee prejudice and natural inclinations, although these were not completely silenced. As early as 1845 Brownson had clearly voiced his antipathy to Nativism. Foreigners, he indicated, should be welcomed to our shores, including "the brave and warm-hearted Irish."[46] The New World should be regarded as a chosen land for the wronged and downtrodden of all nations. Americans should reject those ungenerous prejudices that have no place in such a haven.

Brownson was perhaps too knowledgeable. He understood the major objections that were brought to bear against the immigrants, repeated them, usually supplied a gloss, and succeeded in irritating large numbers of immigrants and Irish-Americans. He did point out one very practical reason for their unpopularity: simply that they did not usually vote for candidates endorsed by the Native Americans. This distaste was exacerbated by two prejudices inherited from colonial days: contempt of the Irish and hatred of the English.[47] And to this must be added the traditional Protestant bias against Catholicism in which the majority of Americans concurred.[48] Brownson protests against this bias in the name of the Constitution and of the good name of the nation. However, he does not give the incoming immigrants *carte blanche.* They ought to be reminded that the right of suffrage is not a natural but a municipal right.[49]

Brownson wrote often and well on the subject but in a way that won the hatred of the Native Americans and the resentment of the Irish. He repeatedly affirmed that an American nationality was a reality of which the population of English origin and descent comprised its heart. Individuals coming from other nationalities must accept the fact that they will ultimately lose their character and be assimilated into the Anglo-American race.[50] Foreign immigrants must realize that a nation is not obliged to admit foreigners to the immunities of natural-born citizens. They would do well not to claim as a right what is only a grant. Although he strongly defended the natural right of the nation to guard against any threat to its identity,[51] he did not hesitate to take a vigorous stand against the Know-Nothings birthed by the Native Americanists, as reflected in three articles written during 1854-1855. He denounces them with verve but often falls into a sort of condescension that tilts to the humorous, as when he adds to the defense of the poverty of most immigrants, the addenda: "without a similar population... who would do our dirty and disagreeable work."[52]

No doubt, Brownson was ambivalent. On the one hand the immigrants were fellow Catholics who had entrusted themselves to the protection of the United States As such, they should be defended on both religious and patriotic grounds. On the other, their radicals and underclass constitute a clear and present danger. Brownson also thought that

Catholicity would be successful in the United States, perhaps even to the point of conversion, only when the Church became truly American. The continuing waves of immigrants delayed the process. Added to this, his often unpleasant dealings with Irish American prelates and journalists and his own deep Yankee prejudices did not make for easy sailing.

During the period covered in the present chapter two issues are in the forefront, that of Native Americanism, which reaches its peak in the 1850s, and that of slavery, which builds to a climax in the conflagration of the Civil War. Brownson castigates both while remaining tractable insofar as particular circumstances are concerned. Slavery is a moral evil but not *malum in se* and should, as disposed by law, be tolerated for the present. Know-Nothingism is an evil grounded mainly on irrational prejudice but is nevertheless correct in some of its assumptions. Leroux's theory of communion is again adopted, with reservations and future expectations. He wavers on the subject of Catholicity and the Spirit of the Age, at first excoriating any attempt at rapprochement, marking the perils it entails. Then, in less than a decade maintaining that a new democratic order is inevitable and should be welcomed. Brownson continues to vacillate, searching perhaps for a center in which his turns and reversals can find their resolution.

IX

War and Recollection

In the years immediately before the Civil War, Brownson began to move toward a more liberal position, provoked by European moves against the U.S. and other factors, including his bittersweet experiences within the Catholic fold. He had already returned to his pre-conversion philosophical mode, recovered his admiration, if not enthusiasm, for Leroux and Montalembert, and was exposed to novel intellectual stimuli, all of which stalled his movement toward conservatism. He came to believe that many members of the Catholic clergy considered manliness and independence as the near equivalent to heresy and schism, or, as he stated tartly, even worse, anti-Irish.[1] By 1860 he was suggesting, counter to his previous view, that Catholic philosophy be reconstituted to fit the intellectual needs of the day and philosophy detached from theology. The passion for change had become too strong to resist.[2]

This only a year after Theodore Parker had taken him to task for being "perhaps the ablest writer in America against the Rights of Man and the welfare of his race."[3] Brownson was obviously retreating from this position, if he had ever held it. Moreover, he was still convinced that if Catholics were exposed, in everything but religious services, to Protestant attitudes and assumptions, they would soon be Protestants in all but name. About this time, he wrote Father Hewit (Father Hecker's friend and successor as head of the Paulists) that he followed a certain method in his study of Protestantism: "first to ascertain, not the errors, but the truth it still maintains, and to show that the truth can find its unity and integrity only in the Catholic Church."[4] This method is very much like that used by Father Hecker, and applauded by Brownson, in his *Questions of the Soul*.

New York had not proven to be a haven. His relationship with Archbishop Hughes progressively worsened. In 1856, when Brownson gave the commencement address at St. John's College (Fordham), he was obliquely attacked by the archbishop because of his views on the Americanization of the Catholic Church. Hughes had no sympathy with his belief that Catholic progress in the U.S. would be enhanced when immigration diminished, nor with his general optimism regarding national conversion.[5] Although Hughes professed to be well disposed toward Brownson and most likely was when it served his purpose, this intent was often belied by his actions. The archbishop later censured *Brownson's Quarterly Review* for its militant tone and advised Brownson to stop ventilating the question of Americanizing the Catholic Church in the United States. In turn, Brownson was hardly edified by the Archbishop and the menage that surrounded him. This group included William Seward, later Secretary of State under Lincoln, and less respectable figures such as Thurlow Weed, a Whig political leader of dubious reputation. When Hughes went to Europe to negotiate a loan for the diocese, he took Weed and Bishop Purcell, another Brownson critic, in his entourage.[6] To escape from the oppressive atmosphere of the archbishop's domain, Brownson moved with his family to Elizabeth, New Jersey in 1859.

Brownson continued, perhaps unwarily, to augment the friction by publishing articles criticizing the parochial schools, pointing to the encouragement they afforded immigrants to avoid assimilating. The archbishop's journal, *The Metropolitan Record*, countered by publishing *Mary Lee* in serial form, which parodied Brownson as Doctor Horseman, a spectacled, dogmatic, tobacco-chewing, harsh-voiced Yankee, contemptuous of the Irish. Someone, perhaps Hughes himself, must have intervened, because when *Mary Lee* was published in book form, this character underwent a surprising transformation into the mild Doctor Henshaw.[7] Nevertheless, Hughes's antipathy toward Brownson appears to have influenced the Jesuits, who compounded the crudities he was subjected to at Fordham with an additional incident at Boston College. He was asked to leave even though he was only making a social call on Father Gresselin, who at one time had been his confessor.

Brownson reacted predictably, accusing the Jesuits of disloyalty to the United States, the very charge launched against him at the time of his conversion and later during the Americanist controversy. The Jesuits are under the authority of a foreign superior and are "not adapted to our age, and especially to our country."[8] Though these criticisms have been ignored by several authors, including Father Ryan, there is no doubt that Brownson did harbor a good deal of animosity against the order. He accuses them of having outlived their usefulness and having made theology into a dead science, faults the *Spiritual Exercises*, compares the Jesuits to the barren fig tree of the Gospel, and supports Gioberti in his controversy against them. It must be said, however, that Fordham, perhaps as a belated "mea culpa," awarded Brownson his first honorary doctorate, a doctor of law, and today harbors the Brownson memorial bust.

Both the Archbishop and Brownson were aggressive, dominating personalities. They were bound to clash. Brownson believed that Hughes had taken unfair advantage, untowardly crushing him with the weight of episcopal authority in a matter of simple opinion, and resented the slights and reprimands he had been subjected to. Hughes was a courageous and valiant man but very much an autocrat. He was accustomed to the Byzantine twists and turns of political maneuver and was burdened with the failings peculiar to the immigrant church. In addition, the archbishop believed that Brownson belonged to a party of Americanizers who were frankly disloyal. He considered that in teaching that Catholicism and the American Constitution fit each other as key to lock, they might eventually succeed in corroding Catholicism and putting it at the service of Americanism.[9]

However much his sympathies took him in this direction, Brownson was not involved directly in groups that had been formed to Americanize the Church in the sense of liberalizing it, although doubtless friends were so involved. A few years later, in a letter to Cardinal Bernabò concerning Brownson's case being heard at Rome, Archbishop Hughes faults him with unfortunate articles, false speculations, bad writings, and refers to him as a free thinker with strong connections to disloyal priests. He cautions the Cardinal: "I don't think it would be very useful to open up a debate with Mr. Brownson. He likes to argue."[10]

Brownson began to suffer from gout, an affliction that proved to be long-lived and extremely painful. Father Hecker, always considerate but often slightly addled, referred him to a physician, converted to Catholicism, who believed that his treatment for gout had been inspired by the Holy Spirit.[11] It consisted principally of bleedings and large doses of whiskey, the second part of which would be taken up with enthusiasm.

Hecker was beginning to emerge from his discipleship after his unfortunate sojourn with the Redemptorists, expulsion, and later founding of the Society of St. Paul. He adopted much of Brownson's early thought, especially concerning the providential role of American Catholicism, to which he became extremely attached. His fervor increased even after Brownson's enthusiasm began to wane. Other points of disagreement included the extent of the ravages produced by original sin and the possibility of adjusting Catholic teaching to the taste and temper of a nation or historical epoch, with Brownson fluctuating on the second question. He was to undergo a surprising disenchantment with the American character, finally coming to the conclusion that "there is scarcely a trait in the American character, as practically developed, that is not more or less hostile to Catholicity."[12]

However, in pre-Civil War days, Brownson was sanguine. He boasted that he had resumed his personal identity, "reunited our present life with our life prior to our conversion."[13] Always given to mercurial enthusiasms, he became an advocate of Gioberti, an adversary of the Jesuits, who had taught that the Roman Pontiff, to recover his true spiritual supremacy, must lose his temporal power. In a typical burst of extravagant exaggeration, Brownson praises Gioberti as superior even to Plato "in grasp of thought, natural grandeur, science, erudition, and intuition."[14] He then proceeds to ride roughshod over Aristotle and Descartes.

The Abbe Gioberti was one of the major stimuli prodding him in a liberal direction. In *Il primato morale e civile degli Italiani* he maintained two propositions that Brownson would enthusiastically support. First, that there is no necessary antagonism between the Church and the world. Second, there should be a progressive agenda to reconcile Church and world.[15] Brownson wrote several monographs on Gioberti's thought and defended several of his theses including the formula "*Ens creat Existentias*" as the *primum philosophicum*. In one of his more extraordinary exaggerations he went so far as to state that before the Giobertian formula "philosophy was not and could not be a science."[16] Even when Gioberti was in disgrace, due mainly to his lengthy attack on the Jesuits in his *Jesuita Moderno* and Rome's condemnation of ontologism in 1861, Brownson still held him in high esteem as a philosopher.[17]

What Brownson had in mind was somewhat less complex and theologically suspect than a simple examination of the formula would suggest. It expresses the real relation between God and creatures—Being and existences—as expressed by the creative act. *Ens*, or God, is real and necessary Being. Whatever is contingent depends on the creative act and exists only by virtue of that act. All truth then—of being, of existence, of relation, is embraced by the "ideal formula" of "*Ens creat Existentias.*"[18] Perhaps the principal difficulty resided in Brownson's notion of intuition that appeared to place him in the camp of the condemned ontologists. But for him intuition was indirect, indefinite, and must be subjected to the work of reflection so as to affirm that *Ens* is God.[19] As will be noted a decade later, under different circumstances, Brownson gave his last and perhaps best summary of his reading of Gioberti's thought. By this time his enthusiasm had waned: "there is less originality in Gioberti than I once supposed.... I do not rate him as high as I at one time did."[20]

In what son Henry calls the most humble passage ever penned by his father, Brownson wrote in retrospect:

> For four or five years, ending in 1864, I listened
> with too much respect to those liberal or liberaliz-
> ing Catholics.... My faith was firm and my confi-

dence in the church unshaken, but I yielded to what seemed at the moment a wise and desirable policy.[21]

This new turn had been announced by articles such as "Liberalism and Socialism," and "Rome and the Peace," in which he proposed that the current threat to society was coming not from democratic license but from an excess of authority. To Montalembert he wrote: "I think I shall be here (NYC) more free to advocate our old constitutional doctrines, and I am nearer friends on whom I have chiefly to depend."[22]

Brownson had moved to Elizabeth, New Jersey, where he settled with his family at 12 Pearl Street and found a patron in Bishop James Roosevelt Bailey of Newark, the nephew of St. Elizabeth Anne Seton, and later Archbishop of Baltimore. A convert himself, he appears to have liked Brownson, tolerated his eccentricities, and named him *Ursus Major*.[23] In Elizabeth his physical and psychological ailments burgeoned. There were family quarrels and strained relations with family and friends. Lord Acton, something of a gossip, reported that "Brownson is not yet sixty, and his decay is pitiful and premature."[24] But these reverses did not mute his growing liberalism. Perhaps, as Sveino has proposed, his reading of Gioberti and Montalembert reawakened his former belief in the possible reconciliation between religion and modern society. There is also much to be said for Phillip Schaff's view that Brownson "has still in the bottom of his heart a whole mass of Protestant principles and impulses of independence and private judgement."[25] More to the point was the growing hostility of European nations to the United States, which would later take the form of support for the Confederacy. In any case, many strands, both conscious and unconscious, came together to produce this liberal reaction.

Civil War, 1861 – 1865.

The Civil War began with the bombardment of Fort Sumter on April 12, 1861, and ended with the surrender of General Lee at Appomattox on April 9, and of General Johnston at Greensboro on April 26, 1865. Approximately four million troops took part in the war that resulted in the preservation of the Union, the abolition of slavery, and other important social and economic changes. Twenty-two states were arrayed against eleven Southern states, containing only one quarter of the white population. Three and a half million slaves proved of assistance to the South providing the labor required for the production of food and construction of fortifications. Over two-thirds of the officers and all the men of the old army were on the side of the North. All the manufacturing centers were within its borders, all the shipping in its hands. The South was dependent on it for practically everything except food. However, a disproportionately large number of the ablest men in the old army resigned their commissions to follow the Confederacy, including Robert E. Lee and the two Johnstons. The South, enjoying an aristocracy accustomed to rule, and another class who recognized their claim to their obedience, could boast better and more quickly trained soldiers.[26]

The conflict brought about several changes in Brownson. He still professed a poor opinion of Abolitionism and had nearly as poor an opinion of President Abraham Lincoln. He had agreed with Justice Taney on the Dred Scott decision, though wary of its possible ramifications. Slavery was a question to be solved by the individual states, not by the federal government, which he believed could provide an answer only at the cost of destroying the Constitution. He never veered from the opinion that slavery was morally wrong. When he published his views and predicted accurately the Northern adverse reaction to Southern policy, he was attacked in print.[27]

Like his friend John C. Calhoun, deceased in 1850, Brownson thought it a pity that his party had given up the old name of Republican and replaced it with the misleading name of Democratic, leaving the Whigs free to adopt it. In spite of his gibes at Lincoln, "thick-headed, ignorant, obstinate as a mule,"[28] and his constant dissatisfaction with the government, Brownson was a devoted, an impassioned, Union man. The rebellion must be crushed at any cost. The slave issue was merely ancillary: "it was not liberty for the Black race so much as for the White race that we wished to secure."[29] This again put him at odds with the Catholic hierarchy, as there was a widespread belief that both hierarchy and the Jesuit Order possessed large holdings in the South that they did not want disturbed. He excoriated them as unpatriotic and proposed the *immediate emancipation* of the slaves as a war measure demanded by military expediency.[30]

This firm pro-Union stand vindicated his patriotism, which had been under a cloud since his conversion to Catholicism and the following Know-Nothing agitation. He was again in great demand as a speaker. Horace Greeley devoted a page and a half of the *Tribune* to reprinting a powerful article of his, praising Brownson as the ablest of all the Catholic writers who use the English language.[31] Brownson made several visits to Washington to give lectures. President Lincoln reportedly attended one of them and received him at least once. Because of the war, however, his disenchantment with the Catholic Church reached monumental proportions: "No religious body... stands so generally committed to slavery and rebellion... as the Catholic... we need not be surprised to find it some day made use of to our prejudice."[32] In a letter to Montalembert, Brownson refers to Archbishop

Hughes as "a man whose word cannot be relied on.... [H]e remembers to speak the truth only when the truth serves his purpose."[33] We note the Vermonter's interpretation of the compromises, deals, tradeoffs, and manipulations of New York's premier cleric.

After many humiliations and defeats at the hands of Archbishop Hughes, Brownson finally won a signal victory when he caught the archbishop in an unguarded moment and pointed out that in defending the slave trade, he had incurred excommunication in accordance with Pope Gregory XVI's prohibition of 1839.[34] Henry Brownson suggests that his father believed that Hughes' article had been written for the express purpose of stalling the anti-slavery sentiment of the country and to bring the pro-slavery prejudice almost universal among Irish Catholics to bear in crushing his *Quarterly Review*.[35] Though paranoid tendencies were not absent from Brownson's character, there could have been some basis to his fears. In any case, the archbishop must have been to some extent mortified as he did not again attempt to confront Brownson directly.

His maladies progressed to the point of fantasy, complaining about attacks of gout... in the eyes, head, and teeth. The financial situation of the *Review* again worsened and again he was rescued by friends. Though still combating "gentilism," the imperative to conform the Church to the world, at least in broad lines, Brownson came to advocate the view that those elements of Catholic doctrine that are merely human could be subjected to modification: "the Church must compromise with what it cannot resist, in the hope that by doing so, it may somehow Christianize it."[36] This hope and its accompanying imperative were resuscitated within the Catholic Church in the present century after anti-modernist restraints began to weaken. Small wonder that Father Ryan views Brownson as anticipating language used by Vatican II, and compares "Catholicity, Liberalism, and Socialism" to Pope Paul VI's encyclical *Ecclesiam Suam*, even noting hints of liberation theology.[37] Brownson emphasizes that there exists no intrinsic and invincible incompatibility between modern civilization and Catholicity. Because of this, Catholics should take the state of non-Catholic thought into account.

In this period of his career, Conservatism seems to be a lost cause. Brownson savages Louis Veuillot of *L'Universe*, one time friend and associate of Donoso Cortes, reads Lacordaire, and corresponds with Montalembert. His is not a radical position but a moderate left-of-center stance. After the fashion of liberal French Catholicism he essays some novel speculations and indelicately voices his dislike of the Jesuit-promoted devotion to the Sacred Heart. As son Henry indicates, his father's "unbounded reverence" for the bishops and clergy became a casualty of his own experience of them. Brownson had come to believe that most so-called "good Catholics" cared little for honesty and less for honor.[38]

Spurred on by the loss of two sons and the imprisonment of a third, Brownson grew more critical of the Lincoln Administration. He was not alone in his assessment of the administration as weak, fluctuating, and appallingly wasteful of men and money.[39] In 1862 he assailed Seward for not pressing the war. He despised Lincoln as "weak, ignorant, and wrong-headed—precisely the sort of man to ruin in times of crisis the liberties of a nation."[40] He was extremely suspicious of the war powers that the president was expert in amassing. Brownson was not without naivete. He was an admirer of Secretary of War Stanton and considered that Fremont (perhaps because he felt the charm of Mrs. Fremont) would make a good president. Deciding to try his hands in politics, Brownson ran for Congress for the Unionists in the third New Jersey district. He lost by some 4,600 votes.

The Civil War enabled Brownson to return to national attention, if not to national prominence. He renewed old friendships with George Bancroft and Charles Sumner, who had become an icon because of his abolitionism, monumental ego, and monumental caning at the hands of a Southern legislator before the war. Brownson's articles were widely reprinted and he again was in demand as a lecturer. Unfortunately, his efforts in favor of the war effort and his intimacy with the Republican Party further alienated him from the majority of Catholics, most of whom militated in the Democratic Party. Archbishop Hughes further muddied the waters by writing an article that appeared anonymously, censuring Brownson for his advocacy of emancipation, maintaining that he was in favor of a war to free the slaves, a view much at variance with the truth. As was noted previously, Hughes did not emerge unscathed. When the archbishop produced a letter from Pope Pius IX calling for peace, Brownson immediately branded it as either an outright fraud or a document obtained by means of gross misrepresentation.[41]

This continuous unedifying squabbling was one of the factors that helped diminish the prestige of *Brownson's Quarterly Review*, a situation worsened by attacks on Brownson by the archbishop of Cincinnati and the bishops of Richmond, Wheeling, and Philadelphia.[42] This sparked concern among other highly placed clergy and matters reached a head when Brownson was denounced to Rome, probably by Putcell or Hughes. Fortunately for him, Cardinal Bernabò, the Prefect of Propaganda, was favorably disposed and the charges against him were dismissed. He celebrated by writing "The Church is not a Despotism."[43]

During this period Brownson was not averse to flaunting his liberal credentials. In a remarkable letter to Richard Simpson (May 21, 1863), director, together with Lord Acton, of the *Rambler*, and later of the *Home and Foreign Review*, he wrote:

> I started as one of the *oscurantisti*, because I thought I must and very much against my nature. After I saw the battle must come, I for a long time shrank from it.... I am in it now, for life or for death... unless we can have manliness and freedom within the Church it is idle to hope for any considerable extension without. We must get rid of French narrowness... and effect a separation of Church and State. We must have reform at Rome and by Rome. That old machine which has driven nearly the whole world into schism, heresy, or infidelity must be broken up.... We must have done with the Middle Ages and not leave its partial carcass above ground to infect the atmosphere.[44]

This is a remarkable profession written to a well-known English liberal with impressive credentials and connections. Less than a year before, Brownson had been extravagantly praising the Spanish conservative, Juan Donoso Cortes, as the apostle of genuine liberty.[45]

What was he up to? Was he simply in the grips of his weathercock compulsion, or attempting to find a comfortable niche in all possible worlds? Was it merely a series of ploys designed to allow him to remain in the limelight? Or did he discover a principle of unity able to synthesize a multiplicity of apparent contradictions? Whatever the answer, his slide toward liberalism was precipitously halted by the promulgation of Pope Pius IX's encyclical, *Quanta Cura*, with its accompanying *Syllabus of Errors* on December 8, 1864.

X

The End of An Era

Though Brownson's liberal interlude came to an abrupt end with *Quanta Cura,* his enthusiasm was already beginning to wilt. Many of his conservative views were, to an appreciable extent, still intact. "Liberalism and Progress," written in 1864, shows that in spite of his move to the left, his opinion regarding liberalism—a liberalism of a certain type—had not changed radically. Factors other than the ideological or purely religious had prompted the initial change in his political stance. The hostility of most European powers to the Union, their aid to the Confederacy, and the French adventure in Mexico was interpreted as part of a movement directed against American republican government. Considering the career of the ill-fated Emperor Maximilian and the ambitions of Louis Napoleon, these suspicions were scarcely irrational. Added to this was Brownson's distaste for, and fear of, the French conservative influence, which was pervasive in the American Catholic Church and presented a real danger to its future development along autochthonous lines.

He repeatedly affirmed that the Civil War was not, primarily, a war between Northern democracy and Southern aristocracy. In fact, he was disturbed that the equilibrium produced by these opposing tensions had been destroyed by

the war and the nation left in a state of uncertainty. The Civil
War, he maintained, could be defended only if conducted "as
a war of the nation for its own existence and rights against an
armed rebellion."[1] It would be an egregious error to attempt
to constitute a new South out of the few Union men residing
there and the liberated Negroes, the detritus of society. Such
an attempt would be a curse both to the South and to the
entire nation.

Modern liberalism is destructive insofar as it endeavors to
separate the progress of society from religion. By doing so "it
has sapped the foundation of society, and rendered government save as pure despotism, impracticable, by taking from
law its sacredness, and from authority its inviolability."[2]
When the multiplication of wants outdistances the means of
satisfying them, serious disturbances are generated, which are
aggravated by peculiarities of the American character which
harbors "a littleness, a narrowness, a meanness, coupled with
astuteness and unscrupulousness, to be matched only in the
later stages of the Lower Empire."[3] Brownson's admiration
for Americans and high hopes for the nation was matched by
a realistic, often hard-nosed, appraisal of both. Insofar as
national character-analysis is concerned, a good case can be
made that Brownson should be included with masters of the
genre such as Santayana, Mencken, and Russell Kirk.

Brownson thought that the political order dominant in the
United States was admirable, its failures due to the prevailing
conception of democracy as a form of leveling, and the
absence of Christian faith. This reduces everything to a "low
average" and substitutes popular opinion for truth, forgetting
that the American political order is not democratic but republican.[4] However, though democracy is hardly praiseworthy as
a political form, it is if understood as the end of government—the common good. The South, which did not fall vic-

tim to a democratic leveling, elevated to prominence more able men than did the North. The superiority of the Southern leaders over the Northern becomes a constant theme gaining in intensity as the Civil War is consigned to memory.

Perhaps taking his cue from the South, Brownson again indicates that while equality before the law is practicable, equality of wealth and social condition is both impracticable and undesirable. This is hardly a new idea for him since it dates from the late thirties. But here he adds that an aristocracy is required to furnish the nation with leaders and models for imitation. It provided the South with unity and strength. The Union struggle against the South was not an outburst of popular indignation against aristocracy but was a war waged in defense of authority against popular license and revolutionism. Brownson's self-esteem begins to dwindle. Concerning his own role in history, he remarks: "we are not only doomed Cassandra-like, to utter prophecies which nobody believes, but prophecies which nobody heeds either to believe or disbelieve."[5] At this point he was scarcely sixty years of age.

Several years before this, he had written a rather optimistic piece, "The Church and Modern Civilization," in which he outlined the privileged conditions enjoyed by the Catholic Church in the United States The Church should take advantage of them, especially as the Catholic faith is the only valuable item lacking to the American people. Somewhat naively, Brownson proposes that once Americans are shown that Catholicity consecrates all they most love in the American Order, and dissociates itself from the medieval abuses linked with it by the popular mind, they would "accept" and "obey."[6] This enthusiasm did not wane appreciably until his last years. It had already been zealously appropriated by Father Hecker.

Brownson blew hot and cold over Lammenais. Though Lammenais lost his privileged position, he never quite became a villain and remained a powerful influence. In 1859 Brownson identified Lammenais' gravest error as his identification of Christianity with universal reason. This, in effect, made the consent of the race authoritative in matters of faith and doctrine.[7] It also equates Church and people; more exactly, one is left with the people and no Church. If the universal Church is only the aggregate of individual believers—the Nominalist position—then the word "Church" is used loosely as it excludes both unity and catholicity. The final development of this identification—perhaps Lammenais's goal—is to make the Church human and not divine, "the thing which St. Cyprian held in horror."[8] Brownson is nevertheless edging closer to liberalism. While he never urges the dissolution of the traditional union between Church and State, this is already a *fait accompli* in the United States, and will, sooner or later, prevail everywhere. It will redound to the benefit of the Church. Catholics must come to terms with changes such as this, as well as the inferior status accorded to the Catholic nations by non-Catholic nations who are free politically and lead the world in commerce and industry. They must keep up with the "New Age": whatever forms of error are spawned must be met by new and original expositions of the truth.[9]

During this period he continued to mark the providential conjunction of Catholicism and republicanism. It is imperative, Brownson advises, to maintain the Republic in accordance with the thought of its founders, "by mediating between the authority of society and the freedom of the individual, restraining each from encroaching on the just rights of the other."[10] Wisely, he indicates that extravagant expectations of national conversion should be muted. Though Americans have a proclivity to overestimate nature, they live in a

Christian nation where the natural law possesses supernatural organization in the Catholic Church. This provides grounds for hope. So does the fact that Christian doctrine and tradition were present in the minds of the founding fathers and are still operating on minds outside the Church. Brownson urges that without the presence of the Catholic Church, these strong, positive forces would tend to languish.[11]

He is aware that the Christian System, as he calls it, has broken up, and that a new system has been introduced which has emancipated power not only from the authority of Pope and Church, but from all restraints provided by the moral order.[12] This New Order is independent of religion and morality. It recognizes only reasons of state and expediency as determining factors. This is political atheism. Power is emancipated from all restraints, no longer finding support in either the affections or the conscience of the people.[13] Writing in 1860 he warns that although modern political atheism used to wear a democratic form, it has lately assumed an imperial or monarchical form. In either case, he urges, the Christian is obliged to affirm the supremacy of the spiritual order and of the Pope, its representative.[14]

Yet, even within this liberal hiatus, Brownson has not completely shifted the burden of guilt from the people to the rulers. When he castigates Catholic education for its errors and flaws, he faults the Catholic community while suggesting it is under the influence of an older and fully formed community that is principally to blame. It is a community in the process of formation that would do well to study the present situation attentively to determine which changes are inevitable and which are not, in order to proceed accordingly.[15] Again inevitability is flourished as a convincing argument against non-Americanized Catholics.

The Civil War brought with it as one of its most urgent sequelae the future status of the Negro slave. The two issues were intertwined but not, Brownson suggested, in the way that both the popular and abolitionist press would have it. In 1857, before the outbreak of hostilities, Brownson suggested the real issue between North and South was simply power. The South seeks to consolidate the slave interest to augment its power. The North opposes it to diminish the power of the South and augment its own power.[16] In April of the same year he cites Pope St. Gregory the Great (*Moralia*, 21, 11) to the effect that God did not give man dominion over man, and while agreeing with Justice Taney's verdict, faults his assumption that Negroes are politically and legally a degraded race in the Union. This is not the case: "they may be so in some of the states, but they are not so in the Union, nor indeed in all of the states."[17]

Brownson was deeply disappointed and angered by the Catholic reaction to the Civil War, their lukewarm support of the Union, and evident sympathy with the Confederacy. In October of 1861, he reproved the "Catholic population" for their want of loyalty, indicating that out of a dozen Catholic journals, only two—the *Catholic* and the *Tablet*—are decidedly loyal, while seven are really "secession sheets."[18] He believed that the greater part of the clergy had Southern sympathies and that many were moved in this direction by material interests. He accordingly initiated a defense of the Negro, who he suspected could play an important role in the conflict. We must realize that the Negro is a man, a human being, who "has the same natural and inherent right to liberty as the white man."[19] Two years later, he admonished, "sneer not at the nigger, for today it is in him we must find our Lord, and in serving him that we are to serve the Church of God."[20] In January 1864, he observes that President Lincoln's Emancipation Proclamation was devious in that it "secured plenty of nest-eggs for slavery" because of the exceptions it contained, and demands the utter extinction of Negro slavery. By incorporating the Negro into its armies, the nation has naturalized him: "They are now our countrymen."[21]

These statements should not be taken out of context. Brownson had serious reservations concerning the Negro population of the United States. He considered them inferior to whites and believed, if not assimilated by the white majority, they would be the source of major difficulties. Because of these fears, he supported plans to promote Negro colonization. But with Negro incorporation into the Union army, this was dropped. Colonization had also been a solution advocated by President Lincoln, to whom slavery was only ancillary to the main task of preserving the Union. He wrote the following to Horace Greeley on August 22, 1862: "My permanent object is to save the Union, and is not either to save or destroy slavery."[22] In several messages to Congress and in the act abolishing slavery in the District of Washington, Lincoln endorsed colonization, discussing the possibility of settling the "freed people" in South or Central America.[23] He presented colonization as a feasible alternative to a Committee of Colored Men on August 14, 1862, in an address that was hard-nosed on the point of racial differences:

You and we are different races. We have between us a broader difference than exists between almost any two other races. Whether it is right or wrong I need not discuss, but this physical difference is a great disadvantage to us both... ours suffer from your presence... we suffer on each side. If this is admitted it affords a reason at least why we should be separated.[24]

The President's preliminary Emancipation Proclamation of September 1862 stated that colonization efforts continue. In his Annual Message to Congress on December 1, 1862, he indicated the only countries willing to accept colonists of African descent were Haiti and Liberia.[25] Probably some moves were made in this direction. Lincoln's letter to Secretary of War Stanton (February 1, 1864) suggests as much. He orders a transport to be sent to the island of Vache off the coast of San Domingo to bring back the colonists who wanted to return to the United States.[26]

Brownson's thoughts on the subject moved along the same grooves prior to the induction of blacks into the armed forces. As late as 1862, he believed that it was necessary to end slavery and to persuade the ex-slaves to emigrate to "some tropical region congenial to their constitution and temperament... leaving the whole territory of the United States to the white race."[27] This would serve two purposes: it would weaken the slave-power and prevent the "Africanization" of free American society.[28] Like Lincoln, Brownson's opinion of the black race is decidedly adverse. The African race is the most degenerated, the Caucasian the least. Though accepting the original brotherhood of the human race, he does not concede the present equality of the races, "or admit that the two can form in the present state of their respective development, society together."[29]

He continues to denounce the moral depravity of slavery and the slave trade, condemned by the Church in spite of Catholics being counted among the principal slavers.[30] He recalls John C. Calhoun's admission that the relation between master and slave is indefensible but balks at arming Negroes and placing them in the army on an equal footing with white troops.[31] His solution: they should be led to full civil freedom gradually, by stages, beginning as *adscripti glebae*, or wards.[32]

The draft riots in New York, in which Irish Catholics predominated, elicited a vigorous but prudent reaction from Brownson, trying to disengage the Catholic Church and the majority of Catholics from responsibility for its depredations. The rioters destroyed the Colored Orphan Asylum, murdered Negroes, and rifled and demolished their dwellings. He was convinced that the riots had been led by Copperheads—Democratic leaders—and planned with the purpose of creating a diversion in favor of the Confederates.[33] It was an extremely delicate situation as the riots generated a good deal of hostility against the foreign-born, the Irish, and the Catholic Church itself. Brownson caustically berated the participants:

> Not having the feelings and associations of our old American born population... to them it is much the same whether they live under the stars and bars or under the stars and stripes, since they were born under neither.[34]

Even the Pope's appeal for peace, publicized by Archbishop Hughes, was dismissed, as previously noted, in a cavalier fashion. The Pontiff cannot require a nation to surrender its rights and dignity and voluntarily consent to dismemberment.[35] He counsels that a wholesale condemnation is not in order. The participants do not represent the Irish Catholic majority.

The principal reason for Brownson's tilt toward liberalism is clearly stated in this October 1863 article concerning the draft-riots. Secession was concocted with the approval of France and England. Its purpose was to destroy republican-

ism in America and deprive the New World of its ability to
influence the Old World through the medium of European
liberals. Most European Catholics, he believed, favored the
Confederacy, except, "that small band of Liberal Catholics
whose organ is *Le Correspondant* and whose leaders are the
Bishop of Orleans, the Count of Montalembert, the Count de
Falloux, Augustin Cochin, and a few others."[36] Convinced of
the existence of a conspiracy against the American Republic,[37] Brownson was quick to launch a counterattack requir-
ing a return to positions that he had previously discarded.

His move to more conservative positions was broadcast by
several works, some of which have been already noted. Aug-
menting these positions is "The Federal Constitution," in
which he returns to a theme essayed some years before under
the inspiration of de Maistre and doubtless influenced by
Calhoun. Here Brownson reiterates his former view that constitutions are generated, not made; the original constitution is
antecedent to its written instrument. Regarding the United
States, the fundamental constitution is that of the people
themselves, as distinct states united.[38] Individual citizens
enjoy political power only as citizens of a state, and of a state
only as a member of the Union.[39] His imagination takes a
Gothic turn when he says that the "mystery of the state" *vis-
à-vis* the race is analogous to the "mystery of the Church,"
and may even be a lower phase of the same mystery.[40] Is he
hinting at the existence of a political mystical body in some
way related to the mystical body of Christ, perhaps function-
ing as its shadow? In any case, it is a refutation of the nomi-
nalistic penchant for dismissing everything not individual to
the outer darkness of unreality.

Nearly seventeen years before "The Federal Constitution," Brownson had been inspired by de Maistre to write:

> The constitution is never made, or drawn up, by
> the people with deliberation and forethought, but
> is always the work of Providence using men and
> circumstances to effect or express his will, but that
> it can never be essentially changed by the people or
> the nation, deliberately or otherwise, without the
> destruction of the nation.[41]

This fundamental constitution provides American nationality with an objective ground and guarantees the nation the necessary protection to contain the whims of the majorities.

Studied attentively, Brownson's liberal interlude, as we have seen, was not a wholesale retreat from conservative positions. It was more of a strategic withdrawal from advanced positions, leaving the bulk of his forces still entrenched in their fortifications. Brownson found himself agitated by unsettling realities such as the Civil War, the Negro question, the draft riots, and the recrudescence of European designs on the New World. Though his strong Union stand enabled him to recover some of his former popularity nationwide, together with his support of Emancipation, it lost him a measure of support within the Catholic fold. But at least the accusations of disloyalty, numerous since his conversion to Catholicism, were effectively muted.

During this period, though he moved toward liberalism as an expansive and anti-tyrannical force, he retained his dislike of it as a form of political atheism. He admonished Catholics to comply with the process of democratization—not identified with leveling—and advocated, although indirectly, the separation of Church and State, which is inevitable in view of the breakup of the Christian System. He continued to stress the privileged status of the Catholic Church in the United States and the importance of the providential conjunction of

Catholicity and Republicanism. He flayed Catholic education, Catholic pro-Confederate sympathizers, Irish Catholic
participants in the draft riots, and Archbishop Hughes. While
insisting on the humanity and rights of Negroes, he continued
to mark their inferiority to whites, and looked ahead to the
future with trepidation.

From this point on, Brownson's popularity and reputation
would again diminish, both nationwide and within the
Catholic enclave to which he had become very much a mixed
blessing. He withdrew from society to live as a recluse, almost
hermetically sealed in his house, left to his gout, whiskey,
beef, and, after his wife's death, to the tender care of his
daughter Sarah and maids. *Ursus major* was in frank decline,
no longer a major constellation. Nevertheless, his intellectual
work continued fitfully. Perhaps his greatest work, *The
American Republic*, would be published in 1865. In the
decade or so after its publication, Brownson continued to
write, debate, and bluster, making himself felt to the readers
of several journals, and continuing an ongoing discussion
that ended only with his death.

XI

Nunc Dimittis

In the aftermath of the Civil War, Brownson was faced with the disquieting events associated with the Reconstruction Era. He was reluctant to grant the freed slaves political equality and was opposed to the artificial restructuring of the South proposed by the government. He feared that the freed slave, if not subjected to a process of education, would take on the vices proper to freedmen without discarding the vices proper to slaves. This would assuredly lead to disaster. Prudence advised that complete emancipation be prefaced by an interim period in which the Negroes would be kept under a regime that would approximate serfdom. Like President Lincoln, he hoped that the black race would vanish from America.[1]

The Negro question was responsible for a rift between Brownson and Charles Sumner, whose friendship had been renewed during the war. Brownson observed that Sumner "had nigger on the brain,"[2] suggesting that in the present unsettled situation Southern individualism was required to temper the exacerbations of New England socialism. He continued to predict that Christendom would eventually be established in the United States on a republican basis but continued to despair of democracy as actually practiced. Brownson's poor opinion of President Lincoln had been furthered by the exceptions made in the final Emancipation Proclamation (January 1, 1863) and the President's disregard for the Constitution in assuming Congressional powers. He feared that a precedent was being set which could in time transform the constitutional republic into a centralized one. He had the satisfaction of having his views endorsed by the *Chicago Tribune*.[3]

Brownson's isolation continued as did the depredations caused by his many ailments. Closeted in his house in Elizabeth, his favorite lament became, "I am now nobody." In 1863 he had decided that the *Quarterly Review* should limit itself to questions of the day and avoid philosophy and theology, as these topics had become so volatile. In 1864 publication was discontinued only to be revived in 1872, ostensibly because of a deathbed request from Mrs. Brownson. He usefully employed the intervening years contributing to several journals and writing what is perhaps his best work, *The American Republic*, which has been exploited by many writers on political theory and influenced others, perhaps the most noteworthy being Fr. John Courtney Murray in *We Hold These Truths*.[4] Always a patriot, often something of a chauvinist, Brownson believed that eventually the United States would absorb Canada and the whole of Central and South America, thus greatly extending its providential mission to harmonize Church and State, religion and politics, by conforming both to the reality of the Divine Order. Given his opposition to the Mexican War and filibusterism, he looked for this to take place through the designs of providence and not by means of military aggression.

The Vatican journal, *Civilità Cattolica*, had raised objections to the principle of religious freedom in the civil order. Brownson replied in "Civil and Religious Freedom," which can be considered an adumbration of the decrees of Vatican II, by stating:

All religions not *contra bonos mores*, or incompatible with the public peace... are equal before it, and entitled to equal and full protection. A free church in a free state entails the liberty of false religions no less than the true one... the precise order which obtains in the United States.[5]

Brownson indicated in *The American Republic* that the Founding Fathers had been greatly influenced by scholastic political thought without being aware of their debt. Maynard pithily notes the line of succession: "they derived their ideas from Locke, who had derived them from Hooker, who had derived from Thomas Aquinas."[6]

Jefferson had read Filmer, whom Locke attempted to refute, and Filmer was acquainted with Bellarmine's speculations, which he, in turn, attempted to refute. In fact, Jefferson's copy of Filmer's *Patriarcha* is presently in the Congressional Library. Filmer was Jefferson's antithesis. Laslett states in his introduction to the *Patriarcha*: "Society for him was physically natural to man. It had not grown up out of man's conscious thinking, it could not be altered by further thinking, it was simply a part of human nature."[7] Filmer maintained that the authority of the state is grounded on the natural authority of the father, of which Adam was the type, and enjoyed continuity by means of the principle of legitimacy. Locke was mistaken when he indicated that Filmer believed all princes are the products of uninterrupted succession. Filmer was a high Tory, a subject of Charles I, who taught that the Great Charter was not binding and that Parliamentary acts are by the king's sufferance.[8]

What Locke was to Filmer, Brownson was to Locke, with the great exception that, without advocating monarchy, he attempts to return to certain aspects of society rooted in

Christian tradition. His principal target is Locke's contract theory. Brownson states that man is limited by nature. If the State of Nature possessed no "germ" of civilization, it would be impossible for the transition to society to be a development. It would have to be an entirely new creation.[9] Apart from subjecting the theory to criticism and displaying the fraudulent character of the State of Nature, Brownson takes the argument into new ground by indicating that the authority of government must be *territorial*. Any government based on contract would ultimately be anarchical or absolute. A pure democracy grounded on the belief that the majority possesses the absolute right to govern carries the seeds of the worst sort of tyranny.[10] It is then only a step to political atheism. The imposition of moral obligation by religion is necessary for both the state and the individual. Otherwise, the logic of political atheism becomes fraught with danger, and, if the premise is conceded, unassailable:

> There is inequality, therefore injustice, which can be remedied only by the abolition of all individualities, and the reduction of all individuals to the race, or humanity, in general.[11]

Brownson aspired to emulate the Founding Fathers. What he admired most about them was their realism. The statesmen of 1787 did not attempt to destroy or deface the work of Providence, but accepted it, and went on to organize the government in harmony with the real order. They were inspired by reality, not by theory or speculation.[12]

Moving once more in a conservative direction, Brownson again discussed the negative aspects of democracy, all the while concocting a grand scheme, one that had hovered on the surface of his mind for several years, of writing a definitive work of grand proportions incorporating his speculations on politics, ethics, and metaphysics. It was never realized. However, he excludes the possibility of aristocratic government in America and endorses general suffrage in principle. He continues to champion Catholicity in the pages of Father Hecker's *Catholic World*. His articles are unsigned, a tribute, not to his humility, if to Father Hecker's editorial policy. He begins to move away from the laborious, pedantic, and often convoluted expositions in which he delighted, and adopted a less baroque style, though still far from the stark simplicity that supposedly constitutes the genius of the English language. He becomes less intellectualized, disposed to accept revealed mysteries with simple faith. In a statement which he previously would have objected to strongly, he affirms, regarding these mysteries, that "philosophy may remove some obstacles to their intellectual acceptance, but as a rule we believe it creates more difficulties than it resolves."[13]

Brownson modified his approach to non-Catholics. Previously, he had accepted whatever was good and used this as his point of departure, attempting to show that the conclusions derived from these principles find their fulfillment in Catholicity. At this point, a movement inward takes place, a sort of religious isolationism. In a letter to Montalembert (June 25, 1865) he advises that "We cannot address ourselves to the non-Catholic mind, because in doing so, we lose the confidence of the Catholic public and our credit with non-Catholics for orthodoxy."[14] Whether this sea-change is the result of deliberation, disenchantment, or a nod to the exigencies of political reality, it is a notable about-face. One is tempted to postulate a withdrawal on the intellectual front that parallels his retirement from the world because of his ailments.

We have spoken of Brownson's fears and adverse opinion of the Negro; his opposition to granting him political and social equality, wary of the Pandora's box such a policy might open. Though against the course Reconstruction later took, he had supported the Lincoln-Johnson policy that sought to restore government to whites in the South, a policy vigorously opposed by Charles Sumner.[15] In 1868 he voted for Grant and in 1872 refrained from voting as he could not, in conscience, support either Grant or Horace Greeley. Brownson was at an impasse. After the Union victory brought the victory of Northern business over Southern slave-holding, effective power had passed into the hands of bankers, stock jobbers, money-holders, railroad and other corporations, all of which he loathed. He found no consolation from the Catholic community that, in a burst of temper, he stigmatized as "the least reasoning, the noisiest, and the most unscrupulous class of American citizens."[16] The irrepressible Yankee temper was still very much alive.

Brownson, in Schlesinger's words, "became a bitter man, wrote on order for the *Catholic World* and had to defer to younger men like Isaac Hecker and Augustine Thomas Hewit."[17]

A bitter draught indeed! A man who was accustomed to being treated as a seer and lionized, reduced to the role of an apprentice writer, dependent on the judgment of two priests whom he must have considered as at best intellectually mediocre. His former glory faded, he was confined to the house, prevented by ill health from fulfilling his religious duties, subjected to constant bickering, and distressed by the loss of his extraordinarily compliant wife Sally, who died on April 9, 1872. Brownson became a caricature of what he once was. He attempted to console himself with meat, whiskey, and prayer. If we are to believe his daughter Sara, he became a rather obscene *Ursus Major*, dirty, unkempt, odiferous, more gruff, loud, and contentious than ever. But as Sara was somewhat unstable, perhaps her complaints should be taken advisedly.

His friendship with Father Hecker, which had weathered the storms of three decades and more, began to show signs of strain. The old disagreement concerning the effects of original sin was exacerbated by the thrust of Paulist apologetics that, in Brownson's opinion, was infected by naive optimism, but the proverbial straw was practical. Brownson had become a major contributor to *The Catholic World*, second only to Father Hewit, who acted as censor, a post that he at first exercised benevolently, but later more strictly. Or such was Brownson's view. When Hewit rejected two articles of his while publishing pieces of his own that Brownson considered ill-considered and possibly heretical, matters reached a head. In 1872 he discontinued writing for *The Catholic World*. He continued to contribute during his last years to the *World*, *Ave Maria*, and the *New York Tablet*; some of these pieces were of a surprisingly high quality given the unfortunate turns taken by his life.

He again asserted *Extra Ecclesiam nulla salus* in a strict, uncompromising manner, reversed his later more favorable opinion of Newman, and, in an unusual move, attacked feminism, female novelists, and the feminine gender in general. A popular Catholic writer, Sister Mary Francis Clare, whose *Hornhurst Rectory* Brownson had reviewed unfavorably (in the same issue in which he praised his daughter Sara's *Gallitzen*), observed, "I fear your feeling against any woman (except one) who holds a pen."[18] This was a crochet of advancing years. As a young man he possessed a truly exceptional empathy and appreciation of women, especially attractive women of intellect such as Fanny Wright. Even then, however, he was repelled by ugly, assertive, masculine women such as Margaret Fuller and Harriet Martineau.

Over the years many of his correspondents were women of wit, intelligence, and independent mind. Miss R. A. Taylor, an enthusiastic advocate of women's rights, had no compunction in writing (May 10, 1842): "women will yet reign triumphant. We shall have you 'lords of creation' all under our thumbs yet." With perceptive irony, she scores "people of sensibility" as "those with the shallowest of feelings, impertinent and obtuse."[19] Another, Miss Anne C. Lynch of Providence, Rhode Island, draws the following tongue-in-cheek impression of Emerson (April 18, 1840): "a very charming man, but of his intellect and reasoning powers I have no high opinion... listening to one of his lectures affects me like the music of an Eolian harp, beautiful but vague, without connexion or point; one recollects the delightful impression without being able to recall the strain of the one or the idea of the other."[20]

Though Brownson grew old and crusty, he still enjoyed the attention of attractive women whenever it was lavished on him. His favorite targets were female novelists, who, he believed, emasculated thought, enervated the mind, and fostered weak sentimentality. He also faulted them for lowering the respect which women were entitled to. Brownson added to Burke's exclamation that "the age of chivalry is dead" when Marie Antoinette was led to the guillotine, the rider that women themselves were largely to blame. Yet he was an admirer of George Sand and Lady Georgiana.[21] He did frown on feminism, believing it to be simply the latest port-of-call of that radical mentality that previously had found its *metier* in abolitionism. As to the clerical *Catholic World*, he peevishly remarked that it housed too many feminine writers, "whether they wear skirts or breeches."[22]

Brownson was, on the whole, disappointed with his children, perhaps unjustly so. Henry Brownson became a writer, an editor of his father's works, biographer, and translator of Balmes' *Filosofia Fundamental* and Tarducci's *Life of Christopher Columbus*.[23] Ned and William fell in the Civil War. Sara became a novelist of some repute and died the same year as her father. Orestes, Jr., something of a romantic, went to sea as a youth, edited a chess review, and wrote popular melodramas. Brownson, after his wife's death, was not the commanding authority who discussed Kant's *ding-an-sich* with his family at the dinner table. Schlesinger paints a somber portrait of Brownson, "half-blind, deaf, smelling of tobacco, and dosing himself with medicine to quiet the gout, drinking whiskey liberally, playing solitary games of backgammon, playing his right hand against his left."[24] Moreover, as he feared death, he forbade the mention of wills in his presence.

Yet he had not quite given up the ghost. He flirted with the maids and needled the rather prim Sarah, suggesting that he had decided to remarry... one of the maids. Closeted at home since 1869, he could assist at Mass only infrequently, receiving communion during a period of some years only twice, both times at home.[25] When Sarah married and moved away, Brownson lived alone with his two maids, whom he called his "secretaries." Every night at nine the three would recite the rosary. After six months he again lived with his daughter and her recently acquired family. In spite of his poor health and advancing age, he revived *Brownson's Quarterly Review*, the first volume issued in January 1873.

During his last years, Brownson hardened in conservative orthodoxy. At this time, Father Hecker, supported by the prospering family business, was using *The Catholic World* for the propagation of what Henry Brownson sarcastically called

"the new Catholic Church."[26] Brownson reacted by continuing his tilt toward ultramontane conservatism. He resumed
his polemic against popular democracy, insisting it was simply the logical political development of Protestantism, and as
such, unfavorable to Catholicism.[27] He had repeatedly stated,
often perhaps with some trepidation, that he had come to the
Church in 1844 not to reform but to be reformed. He was
convinced that the time demanded a strong, manly Catholicism, not an anemic caricature. But he also again turned his
wrath on his Catholic brethren.

He lambasted the Catholic colleges of the day, marking
their failure to teach philosophy in a rigorous manner, send-
ing their graduates into the world "without the philosophical
principles that either enable them to grasp religion in its unity
and Catholicity, or to defend it logically against the heterodox philosophy of the day."[28] He was right then and would
be right today, when scarcely a voice is heard in the ruins of
Catholic education. Brownson inveighed against "the present
infidel movement" which was attempting to abolish the
Greek and Roman classics and transform education into a
purely utilitarian, materialistic, and atheistic enterprise. He
faulted the "so-called middle class" as the chief supporters of
heresy and the bitterest enemies of Christianity—inborn
Protestants, commercial worshippers of Mammon. Here, at
this late date, we find the fire of the Universalist preacher and
the vitriol of the socialist reformer melded with Catholicity,
and emerging with added vehemence.

Though old and feeble, Brownson still aspired to do great
things for God and Church, perhaps to accomplish for his
epoch what St. Augustine and St. Thomas Aquinas had
accomplished for theirs. He strove to establish Christianity
on a firm basis and to struggle manfully against its enemies.
Surprisingly, he still possessed the mental flexibility necessary

to broach a new subject, the philosophy of the supernatural, even after he had moved to Detroit to end his days with son Henry and his family. The supernatural order is seen to flow from the Hypostatic Union, then radiating outwards in creation. A first article on this complex and esoteric theme was published in the 1876 issue of the *American Catholic Quarterly Review*.[29]

To the credit of the clergy, both Father Sorin of Notre Dame and Father Thebaud of Fordham offered to provide Brownson with a residence after the death of his wife as did Seton Hall College, where he had taught for a brief period. He refused. After he moved to Detroit his illnesses worsened in spite of a comfortable room and the attention of his favorite daughter-in-law, Henry's wife Fifina. Orestes Brownson died in character, piously, three days after having engaged Henry in a spirited discussion on the nature of the unforgivable sin against the Holy Spirit. He breathed his last on Easter Monday, April 17, 1876, at dawn, after having received the sacraments.

Orestes Augustus Brownson was buried in the Catholic cemetery of Mount Eliot in Detroit. Ten years later, his remains were transferred to the specially constructed Brownson memorial chapel in the Sacred Heart Church on the campus of Notre Dame. Given the storms and upheavals that have buffeted his beloved Church and nation for over a century since his death, one can surmise that the spirit of Orestes Brownson has not rested in peace.

XII

Final Thoughts

The American Republic has been considered by many, reportedly including Woodrow Wilson, as Orestes Brownson's finest work, though it has vanished from the collective memory of the nation and now must be treated like a precious antique. It was inspired by John C. Hurd's *The Law of Freedom and Bondage in the United States.* Several other influences are also in evidence, including St. Augustine, John C. Calhoun, and the ubiquitous Pierre Leroux. The principal lines of Brownson's thought up to 1865, when *The American Republic* was published, have not been radically modified. Much of it is a rehash of earlier writing but extended and enriched. Universal suffrage is accepted. So is American democracy, now interpreted as *territorial democracy.* Egalitarian democracy is rejected. The providential mission of the United States is reasserted: "the realization of the true idea of the state, which secures at once the authority of the public and the freedom of the individual."[1] This goal is enhanced by the unique character of the American Constitution, which has absolutely no prototype in any past Constitution.

Brownson rejects the state of nature. Its proponents, he urges, are not certain that such a state ever existed in the past and, as to the present, their example of sovereign nations is hardly convincing. The state of nature is merely a convenient fiction to combat Filmer and his advocacy of the divine right of kings and ground sovereignty on the consent of the people. In Brownson's opinion man is always found in society and society is nowhere found without government which strives to combine men "in one living body… to develop, strengthen, and sustain individual liberty, and to utilize and direct it to the promotion of the commonweal."[2] The most natural state of man is to exist in society. Society is a living organism not a mere collection of indviduals. In addition, the state of nature philosophers did not contemplate the existence of territorial states, of nations fixed to the soil, which is the status of all civilized nations.[3]

The doctrine that princes derive their power from God through the people is buttressed by citations from Pope St. Gregory the Great, St. Thomas Aquinas, and others. The people are not the source of political authority as they are in the contract theory, but rather the medium by which it is expressed. Though Brownson agrees with democratic theory in vesting authority in the people, authority emanates not from the people but from God. Moreover, Brownson views the people collectively, not individually, as an organic people, fixed to a given territory. He is describing not mere population but people understood in the republican sense of the word "nation."[4] The exclusion of God from the state, which has for the past two centuries become routine, must be rejected. If divine authority is dismissed, the scaffolding on which civil authority rests is obliterated and can sustain itself only by brute force. For this theory stipulates that authority is derived from God through the people, and guarantees both stability and progress.[5] The connecting link between God and the people is the natural law, which is transmitted through two channels: reason and revelation.[6]

Brownson proposes that the key to modern history resides in the struggle between two constitutions, one providential and foundational, the other having its origin in law.[7] The United States is no exception to this rule. Here also are two constitutions, the unwritten and the written. The former is the authentic constitution of the American people as a sovereign community. It is providential and born with the nation, not made by it.[8] The nation must exist as a historic fact before the existence of the written constitution, before law.

The United States was one sovereign people even before independence. It existed under English common law, distributed into distinct states. Later, the Declaration of Independence was not made by the states severally but jointly as the United States.[9] In a move that betrays residual sympathy with the states-rights theory he had previously endorsed, as well as continuity with his more recent view marking secession as state suicide, Brownson remarks, "the American States are all sovereign United States united, but, disunited, are no states at all."[10] In other words, the organic or territorial people exist only as the United States. The Union and the states are born together, are coeval, and can exist only together. The existing division of power is not that between a national and a state government but that between a general and a particular government. The sovereign is neither the central government nor the states taken severally, but the United States in convention.[11]

In spite of Brownson's progressive disenchantment with his old icons, and his deft, often acid, critique of American and Catholic foibles, the United States is still his model republic, as much as Rome was in its day. The American Republic signals the beginning of a new and more advanced order of civilization. It is ordained to complete and continue Greco-Roman civilization in the political order.[12] But it must be on guard against the corrosive influence of an irresponsible and ever shifting majority that has already added to the fragility of the American order. This is compounded by the unfortunate tendency of the American people since 1825 to view their government as a democracy pure and simple and so to shift it from a territorial to a popular basis. This is opposed to the American tradition and sows the seeds of destruction that can put the very existence of the state in jeopardy.

The two principal dangers to the American Republic are Jeffersonian democracy, categorized by Brownson as basically pure egotism, and humanitarian democracy, as it dispenses with geographical limits.[13] Of the two, humanitarian democracy is the more dangerous. It can pose as Christian philanthropy to persuade the world that humanitarianism is Christianity, and that man is God "sacrificing the rights of men in a vain endeavor to secure the rights of man."[14] Influenced possibly by Donoso Cortés, Brownson insists that political principles are grounded on theological dogma. It follows that if the United States has a political destiny, this destiny must be inseparable from its religious mission.

Regarding the separation of Church and State that he had favored, Brownson does an about-face, suggesting that were the Church to approve the total separation of Church and State it would doubtless be interpreted as a sanction of political atheism. This would be most unwise as it would, in effect, provide the State with *carte blanche* to govern by whim in total disregard of the law of God.[15] In any case, in the United States the State was organized, perhaps unconsciously, in accordance with Catholic principle. This might preclude violent altercations between State and Church. The religious mission of the United States is to let both "move freely, according to its own nature, in the sphere assigned it in the eternal order of things."[16] An ancient Roman would have recognized and approved of his view that fidelity to the American mission may be rewarded by territorial expansion and prosperity:

> Let them devote themselves to their internal des-
> tiny, to the realization of this mission within, and
> they will gradually see the whole continent coming
> under their system, forming one grand nation, a
> really Catholic nation, great, glorious, and free.[17]

Brownson returned to this theme some eight years later in "The Democratic Principle." He again indicates that the Founding Fathers designed the American government as a constitutional republic, not as a popular democracy. He recalls a conversation with Calhoun in which the Cast-Iron Man indicated that it was a great mistake for Republicans to take the name of Democrats, because, "names are things, and in the effort to realize the meaning of the name, the party will lose its character, and become what the new name signifies."[18] That Brownson passed on Calhoun's insight is quite a tribute to the intellectual discernment of both men.

After 1865 Brownson settled into a conservative stance that hardened as he aged, with the liberal and radical residues diminishing and rising only rarely to the surface. Or so conventional wisdom dictates. And much can be stated to substantiate this assertion. Brownson's opinion of the French Revolution reaches its nadir: it is an event carried out "by moral monsters with philanthropy on their lips and satanic rage in their hearts."[19] He marks the moderately liberal Montalembert's "instinctive horror" of democracy and his disenchantment with his friend, Père Lacordaire, when he had gone too far in this direction. There is no doubt in Brownson's mind that democracy, if understood as the absolute sovereignty of people, and absolute freedom from restraint, is clearly opposed to the sovereignty of God and incompatible with Catholicity. The fact that the Catholic populations of Europe have been buffeted for a lengthy period by political atheism—the belief that religion has nothing to do with politics—has resulted in many supinely accepting the rule of infidel terrorists.[20] Descartes is fingered as one of the most prominent thinkers to attempt to divorce philosophy from theology (a divorce which Brownson himself occasionally championed) and thereby exercised an unfortunate sway over French minds by his "philosophy made easy."[21] He is more successful in excoriating journalism. It is the curse of the age, can debase but not elevate, concentrate but not mold public opinion. Journalism shares a common premise with democracy: wisdom and power come below not from above.[22] They are both infernal.

Moreover, some of Brownson's liberal views formulated in the 1840-1846 interim are subjected to modification if not revision. The proper remedy for the ills of the day is not, as Lammenais had advocated and Brownson had at one point urged, breaking with the sovereigns and making an alliance with the revolution, but rather cultivating in the Catholic population:

> Those interior habits and robust virtues that will enable them to dispense with the external props and supports of society, and in asserting for herself in all Catholic nations the freedom and independence she has here.[23]

But this is not a return to his former conservatism in the making. He insists that Catholics must come to terms with the fact that the world is again, as it was in time of the apostles, missionary territory.

Brownson continued to have qualms concerning the future of the liberated Negroes and their impact on the American nation. As he had no doubts regarding their inferiority to whites, the plans afoot to integrate them into one community with whites unsettled him.[24] He was certain that the Negro vote would only serve to swell the tide of political corruption;[25] that even more than the German and Irish immigrants, the Negroes would cluster together, form a distinct class, and vote collectively.[26] He believed that the liberated Negroes would gradually be absorbed by "the superior race" and ultimately disappear. However, this was more of a wish than an opinion grounded in fact. Brownson rolls out his old icon of progress to substantiate his view: "He (the African Negro) has ceased to be progressive, and when a race ceases to be progressive, nothing remains for it but to die."[27]

However, as far as the present status of the Negro is concerned, he has shed his blood in the Union armies, and cannot be deported or forced into colonization. It is now his country, too.

Something of a polymath and an editor with a reputable journal to publish, Brownson ventured into new fields, often with checkered results, moving from a chaos of erudition to territories yet unplumbed. This less fortunate aspect of his work was adumbrated by his efforts at literary criticism, which were marked by an overarching moralism punctuated by bursts of extravagant, if not outrageous, opinion. While he skewered Dickens and women novelists, he lauded Webster, placing him ahead of Bossuet and Goethe. He praised Lord Byron, hardly a model of moral rectitude, but was offended by *The Scarlet Letter*, a story that should not be told! In other fields his opinions were equally idiosyncratic though perhaps

detesting

more reasoned. He branded Mormonism as the Synagogue of Satan; Spinoza as the prince of modern sophists; Jeremy Bentham, a pagan; Francis Bacon, a humbug; and not without malice or humor, England as the *refugium peccatorum*.

Though these judgments are harsh, they are graced by a certain piquancy and style, characteristics usually lacking in his literary criticism. Moreover, he often attained a degree of objectivity. In spite of his detestation for Protestantism, Brownson considered Luther a genuine man and no sham, and reluctantly admired Calvin and Knox because of their energetic and uncompromising character. Perhaps, as literary critic, he was also attempting to fulfill the role of censor, an admirable goal, flowing from his spiritual commitment, but beyond the bounds of his appointed task.

Brownson's incursions into the domain of science were often unfortunate, sometimes resulting in a bizarre amalgam of disparate disciplines. Because of his acceptance of the theory of a primitive revelation vouchsafed to Adam by God, common at the time in clerical circles, he came to the conclusion that it was a mistake to equate the savage and the primitive man. The savage is not the primitive but rather the degenerate man. He takes the renowned theologian Dollinger to task for maintaining "that polished gentility originated in disgusting fetishism."[28] Following in the footsteps of Whitewall, Brownson accepted that many beliefs such as existence after death had their origin in a revelation made to the first parents, perpetuated and diffused by tradition. In "La Mennais and Gregory XVI," he provides a brief account of the theory:

> God revealed the truth to man in the beginning, and in that primitive revelation, the tradition of which has never been totally lost with any nation

or tribe, however obscured, mutilated, corrupted or travestied it may have become, is the type of all the religion that have been obtained.[29]

It follows that Adam, although he lost communion with God, was not condemned to complete forgetfulness. Nor did he become a complete savage.[30] Language plays an important part in the theory and provided Brownson with a point of departure for speculation. The corruption of language would affect the corruption of "the ideal," which is to say, it would pervert or mutilate immaterial truth. Because of the fragility of language that acts as a link between God and men as well as men with men, Brownson is able to conclude that the infallible Church is hardly less necessary to the philosopher than to the theologian. As the Church is grounded on the source of intelligibility, it can guarantee the rectitude of language.

Brownson was usually optimistic concerning the course of history. It moves forward under the sign of progress. In his later years he continues to admit that real progress did exist, but restricts it to the period between the sixth and the sixteenth centuries in Europe, and he attributes it to the powerful influence exercised by the Church.[31] He begins to tilt toward the theory that history is also a process of deterioration, a downward, not an upward spiral. As far as modernity is concerned, those apostate nations that reject the law of God and exclude him from the affairs of the world, follow in the path of the gentile nations and are definitely in retreat.[32] This newly minted rejection of progress, never wholehearted, led him to a somewhat naive rejection of Darwinism while denouncing Darwin and Spencer as "greater criminals even than your most noted thieves, robbers, burglars, swindlers, murderers, or midnight assassins."[33] Evolution, he concludes, is compatible neither with religion nor with science. Brownson's residual fundamentalism is at this point very obvious.

Even more abrasive, at least from the viewpoint of present-day feminism, are his views on women. He progressed—or retrogressed—from a surprisingly liberal attitude to one approximating that of a battle-hardened misogynist. He never ceased to admire women graced with feminine charms as well as intellect; as an older man he was captivated by the charming Mrs. Fremont. Nevertheless, by the 1860's, he was opposed to female suffrage, mainly because he believed that the movement for women's rights was part of a revolution, that it was merely the current stage of an ongoing assault on the normative, natural, and traditional. Chillingly dismissive of their claims, he declares that in the United States the sovereign people "has hitherto been adult males of the white race and it is their prerogative to extend or not extend suffrage to black and colored races, and to women and children."[34]

Brownson asks, "If women are enfranchised will it prevent or cure any single moral or social evil?"—clearly believing that it would not. Such a step would, in addition, introduce a new element of discord into the Christian family and contribute to its destruction.[35] At times he exaggerates, as when he faults mothers for the "pernicious depravity" of Young America. Often he is less abrasive, as when he castigates the women associated with the review, *The Revolution*. They aspire to govern not only their husbands but the nation itself and "be relieved of household cares, especially of child bearing, and of the duty of bringing up children."[36] It should not be forgotten that Brownson, for several years, cultivated the friendship of radicals male and female and was admitted into their circles. We can surmise that there is a basis of fact for his observations that otherwise could be dismissed as the fantasies of an aging curmudgeon.

Moreover, he actually praises the Women's Rights activists for their logic, superior to that of most Americans, and for having the courage of their convictions. Nevertheless, he was convinced that woman needed male guidance, as left to her own devices, "she is out of her element and a social anomaly, sometimes a hideous monster."[37] On a deeper level, Brownson cites with approval Donoso Cortes' view that the family—husband, wife, and children—is no less than a reflection within society of the Holy Trinity.[38] Perhaps it was Brownson's zeal in attempting to preserve the Christian family intact that inclined him toward patriarchal severity and kindred attitudes, often expressed in intemperate language.

His last days were spent commenting on the political situation of the United States. Recollections and backward glances are used as points of departure for often acute but usually jaundiced commentary, often prodded by terribly painful attacks of gout. Even after the President's death, he continued to criticize the Lincoln Administration. It was responsible for the terrible and unnecessary waste of life and funds. This was not his only target. Brownson allowed his pique free rein. Horace Greeley was a revolutionist if not a Communist, Reconstruction a greater calamity than the Civil War, Methodists "the most lawless, greedy, grasping, unprincipled, and fanatical of all the sects that curse the country"—all in a single article.[39] He rails against the "madness" of accepting emancipated slaves on a footing of equality, and repudiates government policy along with the 14th and 15th amendments.[40]

Aside from relatively interesting scatter-shooting such as the above, Brownson turned to themes that had been provoking his interest for lengthy periods. He had considered the masses as a possible source of social fragmentation for some time. It now becomes a constant theme. When there is no power situated above the people, Caesarism has already been established, humanity has been deified, and divine sovereignty rejected.[41] His positive assessment of the United States and his patriotism, though muted, are far from being discarded: "Corrupt as our politicians and no small portion of our people certainly are, we know no actually existing government on earth for which we would exchange our own."[42]

Growing more pessimistic as death approached, Brownson began to predict a coming persecution, a veritable age of persecution. Direct, forceful, blunt, and highly opinionated, he looked askance at most religious groups outside the Church. Jews he once called the chief captains of the army of Antichrist.[43] Protestants and philanthropists fared no better. He believed them to be strong advocates of the supremacy of man—in favor of establishing religion, morality, society, and state on a secular basis without reference to God.[44] Opinions such as that of Fr. Hewit, who would extend salvation to well-meaning Protestants, he viewed with alarm—not out of meanness of soul, but because he considered that such latitudinarian attitudes threatened the very substance of Catholicism. The Reformers had denied habitual grace and, in so doing, rejected the supernatural order and moved toward the practical denial of the Incarnation and of everything distinctly Christian.[45] Salvation, given these circumstances, should not be arbitrarily conceded.

The old liberal Brownson had not disappeared. Though he has words of praise for Louis Veuillot after years of invective, it is tongue-in-cheek, as "the dictator of Catholic public opinion throughout the world." And he continues to chastise Veuillot for attempting to identify the Catholic cause with that of the monarchy.[46] Again, while agreeing that democracy tends toward ochlocracy—government by the rabble—he adds that democracy also tends toward timocracy, government by the rich. In an ill-humored outburst not without insight, Brownson severely censures the Southern policy of the government. It has succeeded in converting the Civil War into a war between the races, "which will not cease until the colored race is reduced to political insignificance in all the states."[47] This has not yet been played out. Let us hope that it never is.

Though immured in his house at the beginning of this period and, at its end, living the life of an invalid at son Henry's in Detroit, Orestes Brownson nevertheless authored a major work, expounded his theory of territorial democracy, and delved into the theological roots of the American political order. His view of the French Revolution and popular democracy became bleaker as the danger of political atheism colored his thought. He continues to view the Negro with trepidation, condemning the Reconstruction policy of the government. Several of his principal themes are encountered in a variety of permutations while new areas are broached. Orestes A. Brownson died contemplating the menacing clouds on a horizon he would never see, a mass of contradictions and disparate inclinations that only the God he was about to meet could reduce to a harmonious unity.

XIII

An Improbable Friendship

The signal friendship between Orestes Brownson and Isaac Hecker lasted well over thirty years in spite of marked differences in character, occasional disagreements, changes of fortune, and the vicissitudes of the age. They began as spiritual vagrants, as seekers, optimistic Americans in search of Utopia, aspiring to lay the foundations of the Church of the Future that would eventually establish a new order. Both found refuge in the Roman Catholic Church and then proceeded to take paths, which at first were barely distinguishable, but slowly came to diverge, arriving at slightly different (in some respects antagonistic) visions of Catholicism. Brownson, in spite of his inclinations, both conscious and subliminal, toward liberalism, at the end settled into a conservative, ultramontane position, although not without backward glances. He became a reflection of the age of Pope Pius IX, which lasted, at least in its essentials, until the pontificate of Pope Pius XII. Isaac Hecker, more in tune with the utopian aspirations of his youth, set a more liberal course, was instrumental in generating the Americanist controversy, and adumbrated the Conciliar Church birthed by Vatican II. Their differing views on the effects of original sin moved them toward divergent conceptions of God, Church, and man.

These views would cause major resonances and provoke, in the period of approximately a century, a violent struggle within the Catholic Church that has not yet run its course.

Biographers agree that this friendship was important to both men and of decisive importance to Hecker, at least during the period in which he played *discipulus* to Brownson's *magister*.[1] He enters the picture as a sensitive enthusiast, suffering a multiplicity of physical and psychological disorders, a worry to his close-knit, eminently practical family, a stranger to the cosmopolitan, intellectually sophisticated world that Brownson had serendipitously entered. He is abstemious, priggish, fussy, given to fads, highly neurotic, but withal inclined to the spiritual. That he was able to strike up a friendship with Brownson, in many respects his opposite number, is extraordinary. The quirky Thoreau would have been a more likely companion for either had it not been for his detestation of religion. But when a master in search of disciples meets a disciple in search of a master, the usual laws of association become the first casualty.

The friendship is a tragicomedy from the very beginning, with a streak of sublimated sadism on both sides which adds a certain piquancy to its unfolding. Acting as the young man's unofficial mentor, Brownson recommends that Isaac, as he was familiar with German, should engage in the study of the works of Kant, Fichte, and Hegel! This only served to further confuse him. Hecker then wandered from Brook Farm to Fruitlands to Shaker Village to Thoreau at Concord. There he proposed that Thoreau accompany him to Europe... on a pilgrimage! When he converted to Roman Catholicism and proposed to enter a religious order, Brownson suggested he enter the Carthusians, then the Jesuits. Hecker finally decided on the Redemptorists where, because of severe difficulties in studying, he undertook a program of private theological study. It must have been successful, as Isaac Hecker received ordination from the hands of Bishop Nicholas Wiseman,[2] and became part of a group of Redemptorist revivalist preachers who gave missions in the United States. Their success served to confirm his commitment to the American apostolate and heightened his hopes for the future. Unfortunately, Father Hecker's efforts to establish an American mission house for the Redemptorists elicited an adverse reaction from his superiors. This eventually led to his expulsion from the order together with certain friends and associates. Though separated from the Redemptorists, he remained faithful to his vision. On July 10, 1858, he founded the Missionary Society of St. Paul (Paulists).

For over three decades, Father Hecker harbored great hopes for Brownson, believing he would emerge as a providential figure, the leader of a Catholic Movement that would convert the nation. With his unfailing enthusiasm, he proceeded to elaborate a "new apologetics" in his books, *Questions of the Soul* and *Aspirations of Nature*, proposing to demonstrate "how the dogmas of the Church answer, in a way, to the demands of the intellect, as the sacraments do to the demands of the heart."[3] Brownson reviewed *Questions* favorably, praising it highly. *Aspirations*, however, he criticized marking Hecker's minimalistic interpretations of the effects of original sin. Nevertheless, their friendship perdured. Brownson's first piece after closing his *Quarterly Review* was a lengthy pamphlet countering Brooks Frothingham attack on the Paulist vision of a Catholic America.[4] Moreover, in spite of divergences that would become exacerbated after 1868, Brownson contributed seventy articles to Hecker's *Catholic World*, second in number only to those of Father Hewit.

When Orestes Brownson died, a solemn High Requiem Mass was sung at the Church of St. Paul in New York with Father Hewit preaching the funeral sermon. Many notables were in attendance. Twelve years later, on December 22, 1888, Father Isaac Hecker died. His first biography, written by Father Walter Elliot, a Paulist, became one of the factors that sparked the Americanist controversy.[5] Although the vicissitudes of Brownson, Hecker, and Hewit have been sketched in outline previously, they deserve to be studied in greater detail. Thanks to the efforts of Gower and Leliaert we can appeal to the lengthy and often illuminating correspondence between Brownson and Hecker to complete the picture.

At the very beginning we find the youthful Isaac Hecker attempting to set up a series of lectures for Brownson at the New York Lyceum, in spite of its president's dislike for Brownson's peculiar opinions.[6] This was a reflection of his good will, benign nature, generosity, and willingness to take on burdensome tasks. As for his peculiar talent to attract eccentrics, of which Brownson is but a pale example, Hecker mentions several. There is Dr. Buchanan, supposedly graced with the power of discovering any disease of body or mind. Hecker remarks, "if there is any medicinal remedy, I ought to try it... living out a complaint is a slow process and wretched living."[7] Dr. John W. Vethake, a physician who became a close friend, was a "profound Swedenborgian," hypersensitive to the point that he feels, hears, and sees more than his constitution will allow. Then there is Edward Palmer, a radical Transcendentalist from New Jersey who wrote a pamphlet urging the suppression of money and private property.[8] This is the beginning of a catalogue of exotic ships that would take this route.

Brownson and Hecker exchanged observations, information, and a welter of aspirations and dreams: Hecker was avid and Brownson self-absorbed, both intensely curious with the latter exuding intellectual aplomb. At first Brownson denies the rumors of his projected conversion, changing the topic to the political: his aspiration to beat the "little magician" (Van Buren) and seat the "statesman" (Calhoun).[9] Yet it was religion that obsessed them both and provided a common ground for their friendship. Hecker, initiating a theme he will consistently develop, affirms that mankind, as it becomes conscious of its deep wants, will strive to bring about the realization of the Church, which, though foreshadowed in the past, was lost sight of by Luther.

Brownson urges that the unity and catholicity of the Church must be restored as an outward visible institution.[10] This is the precondition for any further advance. Although Christianity, in his opinion, preaches the same truth as Platonism, it has the advantage of being a body and not merely a theory. Possibly under the inspiration of William H. Channing's Christian Union, which was founded six months previously under the banner of Humanity, Wisdom, and Holiness, Brownson predicts that in the not far distant future all the fragments that compose Christianity will be reunited. Although the ecumenical purpose continued to influence them, Brownson and Hecker soon became disenchanted with Channing.

Perhaps unsettled by Brownson's exaggerated intellectualism, Hecker declared that he "would not reason God out of the universe.... I feel he is ever-present but I know of no solid argument which makes these facts plain."[11] Both approached conversion by similar paths. Both viewed the Church as a means, not as an end—an instrument to use for the advancement of humanity. Brownson stressed the need to work effectively for our age and country; Hecker aspired to bring down the Heavenly Jerusalem.[12] But in so doing, he displays further signs of anxiety, lamenting his inner trials and struggles, stating that his inner life is spent in "continuous conversation" with an unseen world.[13] These experiences echo those of Brownson's childhood and could apply equally well to psychopathology or the lower reaches of the spiritual life. Hecker seems to have believed that he was one of those rare souls gifted with passive contemplation after the manner of St. John of the Cross and St. Catherine of Genoa.[14] Decidedly, a highly impressionable young man.

The hard-nosed Brownson was not impressed. The domain of spiritual contemplation—of mysticism—was foreign to him. He admonished Hecker: resist this tendency to mysticism; do not dream your life away! As Brownson tended to equate mysticism and spiritual luxury, he again chided Hecker a year later, stating "you are liable to receive the truth under a form too subjective, and to mingle too much of sensibility with the objective forms of faith."[15] While Brownson was busy castigating Ripley and his illusory utopia of Brook Farm, Hecker was enthusiastically praising the nobility and exalted status of man's primitive nature. It must assuredly be glorious if the Son of God alone could ransom it. The ascent of man toward God under the influence of Christianity is compared to "the ascension of a released spirit towards heaven."[16]

Asceticism and sacrifice were, in Hecker's view, ways of realizing man's true untainted nature, not of correcting it by providing an opening to grace. Brownson did not agree with this opinion, which became the point of departure for future conflict. He maintained that human nature had been so corroded by original sin that it required transformation by means of grace to restore its integrity. Man's primitive nature had been marred. Father Hecker moves along another route. Though he can contrast the Catholic notion of freedom to the

Protestant, the annihilation of the will opposed to gratification of the will (which would take him in Brownson's direction), he is perplexed by the problem posed by the good found outside the Christian domain. How can one account for all that is truly worthy among the Hindus, Greeks, and Romans?[17] The specter of the Anonymous Christian looms on the horizon.

For the greater part of their lives, Brownson and Hecker were sanguine regarding Catholicism's role in the United States and optimistic concerning the aptitude of Americans for accepting the Church. Hecker articulated their common faith when he stated that if Americans were filled by a lively faith, new ages of belief would spring up on the continent. The task of the Church is to meet and satisfy the wants of man's religious nature: "the affections of the heart are no less unerring guides to truth than the logic of the intellect."[18] At this point Brownson would demur. He would consider it dangerously close to the revolutionary credo: remove limitations and all will be well! For Hecker it followed logically from his view of human nature and minimalist interpretation of the effects of original sin.

In his youth Hecker made an icon of Brownson. The illusion perdured to some extent: Brownson would be the Catholic intellectual leader of the vanguard of a great movement. After several decades and no small disenchantment, Brownson remained for him the "champion of Catholicity" on whom destiny of Church and State rested. Doubtless, Brownson was flattered by this long-term lionizing. But his notion of Catholicity was different from that of Father Hecker. The Church is objective, it proposes truths to be believed and acts to be performed: "it concerns almost exclusively the reason and the will."[19] Although the statement was made while he was under the tutelage of Bishop Fitzpatrick,

Brownson would remain unyielding on this point after he had regained his freedom and returned to his accustomed philosophical mode.

It is not without irony that Father Hecker, the German-American, would become a more impassioned Americanist than Brownson, the authentic Yankee. When Brownson's anti-Nativist writings were raising welts among the Irish clergy, Hecker noted with satisfaction that the American element within the Catholic Church was steadily increasing and eventually would predominate.[20] Brownson, apart from his usual objections against a predominantly foreign clergy with little sympathy for things American, was disturbed by the woeful lack of conversionary efforts by the Catholic Church among Protestants. He believed this was especially deplorable given the widespread discontent that he noted among the Protestant clergy. A Catholic clergy sympathetic to free and independent spirits could reap a rich harvest of souls. Foreign-born Catholics must realize that Americans are capable of intense loyalty but in a different manner than in traditionally Catholic nations, a difference that augurs well for the future. They are loyal to law, not persons, principles, or men.[21] The Church must proceed in a different manner than customary to win them over.

Father Hecker, writing from Rome, where he had been dismissed by his Redemptorist superiors, has lost none of his enthusiasm: "now is the time to prepare the way for the conversion of the American people."[22] Brownson's letter of September 27, 1857, meets the problem head on. There is no Catholic nation in which the laws are as favorable to Catholicity as in the United States. However, the ecclesiastical authorities, because of their erroneous notions about America, have failed to exploit the situation. The Know-Nothing movements have succeeded in creating a distrust of republican institutions in clerical circles, a distrust further augmented by the prevailing French Imperial sentiment. Because of this, the great body of Catholics has become anti-republican. Rome, Brownson urges, must decide whether those American Catholics who aspire to convert the United States without subjecting the nation to a European political system become otiose, should be encouraged.[23] Father Hecker, who had written for the Vatican *Civilità Cattolica*, indicates that his purpose was to show how Divine Providence has, by means of singular events, prepared the American people for conversion to the Catholic faith.[24]

With Father Hecker's return to the United States, the growth of the Paulist apostolate and Brownson's ever present, at times overwhelming, duties as editor, writer, and lecturer, a lengthy period of relative tranquility ensued. However, in the late 1860's, tensions began to appear when Father Augustine Hewit, the censor of the *Catholic World*, sharply criticized Brownson's "The Problem of the Age," affirming that the author not only misunderstood Gioberti, but that his position was dangerously close to that of the Louvain "ontologists" condemned by Rome. This was a sore point with Brownson as he had previously defended himself against a similar accusation. He refutes the charge out of hand and provides a carefully thought out defense that can act as an addendum, superior in many ways, to his lengthy articles on the subject.

Brownson affirmed that we do not intuitively know God in this life—nor even that God exists—but we do possess a direct intuition of Being (*Ens*) under the ideas of the necessary, the universal, the immutable, the perfect, and so on. This is to say, through the medium of the ideas. Subsequently, by means of reflection and demonstration, this "ideal" can be identified with God. He endorses Gioberti's formula "*Ens creat existentias*," insisting that while *Ens* (Being) is identified with God, this identification is made through reflection, not through intuition: "I have never understood the ideal formula as implying direct and immediate intuition of God, or even of *Ens* itself. An intellectual or reflective process was always necessary to identify the ideas in *Ens* with *Deus*."[25]

However much he was irked by the topic of ontologism, it was the old disagreement about original sin that provided the basis of Brownson's disaffection with Hecker and Hewit. He understood their view in the following manner: although because of the Fall the gifts added to Adam's original nature were lost, his original nature was left untouched. In addition, Adam is considered to be the representative, not the real head, of mankind. As genera and species are not real—only individuals are—it follows that it is impossible to transmit original sin by means of natural generation.[26] Brownson's view was that human nature had been severely mutilated. This means that man is always more or less than nature. More when elevated by grace, less when left in its damaged condition. Everything depends on God, even progress. This icon, which had attained quasi-divine status in the wake of the French Revolution, is not the product of human evolution alone. It also depends on God's free gift of grace.[27]

He bristled under what to him was a despotic regime. *The Catholic World* was not organized according to the liberal standards envisioned by Father Hecker for the universal Church. Brownson complained that Hecker required an impossible unity of thought, given the frank diversity of writers and viewpoints. He resented the "mutilation" of his articles and being forced into the role of a schoolboy writing assignments for a master.[28] To further compound matters, he believed that Father Hewit held views bordering on heresy, such as those on original sin and the divinity of the soul, which tilted strongly in the direction of pantheism.[29] In

March 1868, again prodded by the treatment he was receiving, Brownson makes a surprising confession:

> I am beginning to be once more an *oscurantisti*, and can hardly be said to belong to the Catholic (Americanist) movement. I am become a convert to the Encyclical (Pius IX's *Quanta Cura*) and am almost beginning to despair of the success of the American Experiment.

Significantly, he adds, "I think I am turning Paddy. I have lost confidence in my countrymen and become ashamed of them."[30]

A further Hewit article on New England Protestantism[31] made Brownson "a little savage." The Paulist maintained that there exists no good reason to doubt that the old Puritan ministers were saved, provided they were in good faith. If this is so, Brownson parried, what is the use of preaching or writing against heresy? To aggravate the situation, Father Hewit censored two of Brownson's articles, arbitrarily eliminating two delicate points: whatever implied that human nature had suffered a positive moral injury because of the Fall, and whatever was opposed to the spirit of the age. The latter is now regarded by Brownson as "the spirit of Satan, false and mischievous in its essence."[32] On the practical level, he continued to complain of his excruciating attacks of gout, while Father Hecker answered by bewailing his racking headaches. Strange to say, Brownson may have been in the process of changing his opinion of the Irish. In what could have been either a twinge of compunction or a twist of sarcasm, he speaks of the Irish as "a most remarkable people... a wonderful people... the mainstay, under God, of the Church with us."[33]

Pope Pius IX's letter commending the Society of St. Paul was published by the *Catholic World* in March 1869. The editors of the Brownson-Hecker correspondence point out that the expression "*benevolentiae testem*" found in this commendation reappears thirty years later in Pope Leo XIII's encyclical, *Testem Benevolentiae*, of January 22, 1899, which condemned Americanism.[34] In 1869, Father Hecker was overjoyed contemplating the auspicious prospects of his cause. Writing from Rome, where he was associated with the anti-infallibility group surrounding Bishop Dupanloup, he reports "an increasing interest and appreciation of men of all schools and policies in Europe of the principles of our free institutions and the state of things existing in our country."[35] This letter, dated January 30, 1870, is Hecker's last effort to recruit Brownson for the Americanist program. He urges that the existing system, the decadent monarchical establishment, should make concessions of a liberal and democratic nature if only to prevent further revolutionary episodes: "public opinion and the vote of the people is now the practical ruler of all political action."[36] By prudently conceding a larger share of political power to the people and accepting necessary modifications between Church and State, the Church can avoid not only revolution but apostasy. In a preliminary draft, Hecker called for a close alliance between clergy and people and recommended greater freedom in complying with the authority of the Church.[37]

This left Brownson nonplussed—he had lost his enthusiasm and much of his sympathy for the program. He replied in a lengthy letter dated August 25, 1870, opposing the views set forth by Hecker and continuing to endorse republicanism for the United States—although no longer harboring the great expectations of yesteryear. Though democracy is theoretically compatible with Catholicity, it is not so in the practical order, as understood by the people and politicians. In Catholicity, all power comes from above and proceeds from high to low. In democracy the situation is reversed: all power ascends from low to high. Catholicity and democracy are as antagonistic as spirit and flesh, Church and world. The Church supports authority and is steadfastly anti-radical. Democracy demands liberation from all restraints, a sure invitation to license.

Brownson has become disenchanted with American Catholics. The masses are base and rowdyish with the unfortunate proclivity of transforming scoundrels into saints and martyrs. Here he adumbrates H. L. Mencken's views of the American people as suffering from a libido for the ugly. Brownson's prognosis is pessimistic. Catholicism will be impotent when faced by a nationalistic surge. Any harmony between the two will end in the sacrifice of the Catholic idea on the altar of the national idea.[38]

The difficulties between Brownson and the *Catholic World* burgeoned, finally reaching the breaking point. He wrote to Father Hecker that the manifest differences that existed had persuaded him to discontinue his association with the review. Hecker replied with a considerate, if somewhat smarmy letter, praising Brownson and reiterating his friendship and esteem.[39] Brownson replied in kind: "I trust our intercourse is not to be interrupted, but to continue as cordial and friendly as ever."[40] This was their last communication. Brownson remained in the prison of his many infirmities and resentments, Father Hecker in the prison of his incandescent vision. Some years following Brownson's death, Hecker was to recall his friend and mentor's love of truth and devotion to principle, his mettlesome temper and originality: "he was routine in nothing."[41]

XIV

In Retrospect

Orestes Brownson would play solitary games of backgammon, his right hand against his left—an admirable symbol of his life, thought, and politico-religious wanderings. His unsettling changes, irritating ambivalences, and startling variations follow this pattern. A nicely developed and forcefully presented argument would be taken to a satisfactory conclusion, only to be later stymied by a further argument often proceeding from the same premise. Brownson was a short-term philosopher. Given the appropriate time and change in circumstance, his perspective would change—as would his skein of argument. If Brownson's life were to be parceled out between his different enthusiasms and intellectual enterprises, each segment would doubtless have a value, significance, and unity of its own. Unfortunately, viewed as a whole, there are breaks, ruptures, and dissonances. A single Brownson presents more difficulties than any number of personified aspects of his thought, each of which is valuable taken individually.

At first, Brownson used Christianity to advance his social program and concocted a Christ-caricature to order. He then reversed his position to strongly affirm Christ as Redeemer and Savior and insist on the paramount necessity of a new and divine life. On the political front, he at first advocated radical democracy, pushing political equality to its radical conclusions, but he came to believe that this would lead ineluctably to the annihilation of government, property, and family. He made a vigorous effort to extend democracy, then changed tracks and attempted to maintain, as far as possible, the original constitutional framework. He also came to realize that religion, instead of being employed as a democratizing factor, could and should be used as a structural limitation, exercising a degree of supervision over a society that otherwise would gravitate toward chaos. Brownson ended by denying the legal right to revolution and condemning violent revolution as a tool for social progress. He began by endorsing an order which proceeded from low to high and ended by endorsing an order which moves from high to low... from God to man. His search for a New Church led through a series of corridors back to the Old Church.

Under Bishop Fitzpatrick's direction, Brownson, after his conversion, settled into a conservative mold but later reacted against it, advocating that the Church adapt itself to the prevailing ideas and sentiments of the age, only to retrace his steps and denounce this position as heretical. His early socialistic leanings were discarded and socialism attacked as pantheism adapted to the apprehensions of the vulgar. The Universalist doctrine of salvation as a birthright was scuttled and he moved to the opposite pole, proclaiming "*Extra Ecclesiam nulla salus*" with such vehemence that even Catholic bishops were incommoded. Brownson defended his position by stating that if salvation were attainable outside the Church, there would be no valid reason for entering. In spite of his contributing to philosophy, Brownson was hardly an ivory-tower thinker comfortably ensconced within a web of abstractions. As he often stated, his goal was practical truth, an aspiration that may have fueled his proclivity for change but served to keep his feet on the ground and make him a formidable adversary.

We have a lengthy history of Brownson's vacillations, his advocacy and later about-faces on a multiplicity of issues. His enthusiasms flowed and ebbed, usually passing through three stages. First: advocacy, even discipleship. Second: rejection (usually ill-humored) and critique. Third: reevaluation and partial restoration within the Brownsonian corpus. Pierre Leroux is possibly the only philosophical enthusiasm to be exempted from this to some degree, albeit his thought was subjected to extensive modifications. Brownson's views on philosophy, its relation to theology, and the best pedagogical method for its teaching tended to oscillate. His critical analysis of America and the national character, though acute, moved between extremes without attending to the mean. Even Progress, an icon favored from his youth, suffered a drastic reduction from universal historical lodestone to the effects of Christianity on Europe from the sixth to the sixteenth century.

One encounters in Brownson's thought several odd and bizarre views, which a cynic could interpret as signs of psychopathology or intellectual shallowness. His early visions and locutions, intense dislike for introspection and psychological analysis, long-term interest, if not obsession with, spiritism, Satanism, and other aspects of the underside of the psycho-spiritual life must be noted. In Brownson there is a touch of the magus, with its proximity to the hermetic and alchemical. In the *Spirit-Rapper*, Satan is uncovered as the dark center of a revolutionary-spiritist conspiracy. These interests must have influenced his views on evil and on the deleterious effects of original sin. But he might not have erred in proposing that the abominations of the age respond to similar stimuli, and have a common ground.

But often these variations take place within common boundaries set by external circumstance or internal compulsion. This is the case with his views on slavery, the Negro, and reconstruction. Today his early support for emancipation and his ambivalent defense of the Negro appears to be woefully inadequate; at best a half-hearted enterprise which, in effect, it was. Complete emancipation, he believed, should be prefaced by an interim period in which the Negro would live under a regime approximating serfdom with assimilation as the desired goal, and at very best the disappearance of the Negro as a race. He feared that the Negro, if not absorbed into by the greater society, would come to form a distinct class, vote collectively, and swell the tide of political corruption. These fears cannot be dismissed outright. His overriding concern was the survival of the American Republic and when he viewed Reconstruction as effecting the transformation of the Civil War into a war between the races he considered it a terrible augury for the future.

Into this category Brownson's views on the Nativism controversy can be placed. These are greatly relevant today when the flood of immigration, legal and illegal, has produced a violent reaction and become a question of national importance. Before the mystique of the melting pot and diversity, and contrary to it, Brownson affirmed the real existence of an American nationality of English origin and descent. This is the core of the nation which all succeeding arrivals should strive to emulate and be incorporated into through assimilation. While defending the immigrants, he prodded them to assimilate and preserve and defend American nationality against possible corruption. A nation is not obliged to admit foreigners to the privileges reserved to citizens. Naturalization is not a right. Immigrants must accept the fact that they will eventually lose their character.

This view militates against today's public orthodoxy. A good argument can be made that the Civil War destroyed whatever common ground had existed prior to it. This leaves Brownson's American nationality of English origin and descent, at best, a shaky hypothesis. It appears that Brownson's notion of America as a promised land that assimilates different nationalities and reduces them to a cultural unity has been replaced by that of a common trough around which a multiplicity of faceless, and in large part rootless, humanity congregates. Perhaps Brownson's admonitions should be addressed to the current waves of immigration, usually far less suited to American society than were the Irish of the last century, who possessed communal, social, and religious roots.

The common boundaries or regularities in his discourse on race and immigration may serve to present a Brownson characterized by uniformity and moderation. This is decidedly not the case. He usually proceeds by fits and starts, often veering from thesis to antithesis within an indeterminate period. The prime example of this is the dichotomy between Brownson as religious liberal, advocating social reform, religious freedom, separation of Church and State (adumbrating the Conciliar Church), and Brownson as religious conservative, fingering alien ideologies lodged within the body of the Church, fabricating a counter-Church in accordance with the spirit of the age. On the one hand, he points to the dangers of reactionary monarchism; on the other, to the dangers of rampaging popular democracy. In both cases he makes a valiant effort to tilt away from the direction in which the peril was advancing. Both liberal and conservative find in Brownson's thought a well-stocked arsenal for their positions. This says little for his stability, but does not diminish the worth of his efforts to attend to ultimate concerns.

One is tempted to suggest that Brownson's early goal of Christianizing democracy and democratizing Christianity held him in an irreconcilable tension that he was unable to resolve. Louis Napoleon and dreams of empire are presently at most tarnished fantasies of clerical reactionaries. The other side of the coin, alas, is still with us. We have experienced a strong liberal surge in both political and religious domains that, in the Catholic Church at least, is progressively gaining ground. Because of this, Brownson's "conservative" speculations hold unique importance. He envisioned the advance of a socialism presented under a Christian facade and employing the language of the gospel, and predicted that this use of Christian symbol and language to carry a socialist ideology would end by eviscerating Catholics of their memory and open the door to the fabrication of a counterfeit Catholicity. Brownson called for a re-examination of foundational principles to clear the decks of obfuscation. Unfortunately, this evisceration of memory is today a common phenomenon scarcely restricted to Catholics. It has found a potent ally in what Ortega once called the barbarism of technology. The past is yesterday.

There are other Brownsonian themes, such as the "American idea," which begin with tremendous impetus, are periodically renewed, and fade only toward the end. At first, the American idea was democracy, the equal rights and worth of every man as man. The Church of the Future would have its origin in the United States and ultimately lead to a new global order. Later, in his review of Father Hecker's *Questions of the Soul*, the American idea is changed: it merges with realizing the idea of a Christian society. The theme was extended by his distinction between Old and New America, by which he surgically separated constitutional republicanism from ultrademocratic radicalism. Brownson occupied both positions at different times, finally settling for Old America. When he wrote *The American Republic* (1865), despite many disenchantments, he still viewed the United States as the model republic, modernity's analogue to ancient Rome, indicating that the American Republic signals the beginning of a new and more advanced order of civilization. Although his rosy predictions were scuttled toward the end, he did not abandon the hope that the providential mission of this unique people would, with the grace of God, be carried to fruition.

Brownson's role as American critic should not be overlooked in spite of the idiosyncratic and highly charged expressions by which he attempted to describe the nation and its citizens. His Yankee roots and rustic bluntness are very evident (The Brownsons' support of Ethan Allen and his Green Mountain boys was not an idle reminiscence), as is what Channing once described as his morbidly sensitive vision.[1] Though somewhat limited geographically, he cannot be accused of closed parochialism. His travels as a lecturer allowed him to come in contact with much of the country, and gave him a taste of customs and mores different from his own. In spite of the constellation of virtues with which Americans are graced, Brownson believed that the worship of lucre was fast replacing the worship of God. This upset had been caused and propagated by the industrial order that he abhorred, but was able to analyze with expertise, subjecting Locke's notion of property and its later accretions to rigorous criticism. He noted the excessive strength of public orthodoxy, and the subsequent degradation of freedom to the ability to echo the public voice. Brownson contended that this subordination to public opinion, noted by other observers of the American scene such as Tocqueville and Dickens, had adulterated the stern and manly qualities of the Founding Fathers, preparing the way for a fast approaching era of the demagogue.

Among other attributes of the American character, he notes the combination of astuteness and unscrupulousness, an infatuation with the new, the bizarre, and the marvelous, a perverse attraction for the ugly, and a penchant for placing villains in its pantheon of heroes. Although Brownson can rightly be accused of presenting an ongoing meditation on the decline of the United States, this was punctuated by long episodes dedicated to the celebration of the American character and its providential role in history. He praised the independence and personal dignity of the American: his reverence for law, attachment to duty, discipline and courage, and his keen desire to acquire truth, operational truth, truth that can be put to work. He lauded the unique American characteristic of uniting in the same person the man of thought and the man of action, joining philosophical insight to persevering activity. Nevertheless, in spite of the *ad hoc* character of many of his opinions, some corresponding to personal pique or to swings of mood, Brownson was a perceptive diagnostician.

Brownson's speculations on matters religious and political spanned his entire career and ended only with his article on the Philosophy of the Supernatural published the year of his death. He was able to break new ground or probe more deeply into a theme disfigured by age and overexposure. He accomplished both in his development of political atheism with its adjuncts of heathenism and gentilism. Political atheism divorces politics from religion, while heathenism rejects the subordination of the secular to the spiritual, and gentilism aspires to conform the Church to the world. These are aberrations that can arise either from the Right or the Left, conservatism or liberalism, when taken to their radical conclusions. Brownson denounced all three while flirting with gentilism.

The post-conversion Brownson never intended to compromise the integrity of the Christian faith. At most, during his liberal hiatus, he desired to modify those elements that were merely human. Even when advocating the separation of Church and State—already established in the United States—he did not propose the erection of an iron curtain between them, nor the banishment of the Church to the outer darkness of political life. He did propose the termination of those otiose arrangements customary to monarchical Europe that, in his opinion, had served to put the Church in a subservient position. He argued that there is no intrinsic incompatibility between modern civilization and Catholicism (an idea which is currently in vogue) but later, prodded by Pius IX's encyclical, he rejected it together with his vision of a Catholicity assenting to a new order justified by the irresistible wave of the future. Brownson then came to a position in which Church and State complement each other as power and authority. In this view, the State appeals to the authority of the Church and uses its power to enforce the practical determinations made in the light of the Church's wisdom. The worst depredations of modernity have had their point of departure when the State incorporated into itself both power and authority.

Turning to the United States, Brownson maintained that the Founding Fathers and the Constitution were rooted in the medieval tradition of natural law and indebted, although unbeknownst to themselves, to the speculations of the Schoolmen. Americans live in a Christian nation and the natural law, which is transmitted through the two channels of reason and revelation, possesses in the United States a supernatural organization in the Catholic Church. Thus the Christian tradition that operated in the mind of the Founding Fathers also operates on minds outside the Church and continues to do so. However, this influence exercised by the natural law would diminish with the diminished presence of the Catholic Church.

This theme has nourished many later writers, perhaps the most notable being Fr. John Courtney Murray,[2] who defended the thesis that the natural law was the basis of the consensus that unites Catholics, Protestants, and Jews. By a happy accident, the natural law found a better home on these shores than on the continent, tracing its origin to the prominent role it played in English common law. But Murray's notion of a still growing consensus or public orthodoxy, the content of which is one with the natural law, diverges from Brownson's work, by being overly optimistic. It appears to presuppose a consensus which develops automatically, without the strong presence and inspiration of the Church.[3] Brownson feared that a New Order independent of religion would result in the abolition of checks and restraints and end in political atheism. He came to believe that should the Church formally approve of the separation of Church and State, this would be construed as an approval of political atheism and provide the State with *carte blanche* to govern by whim. Today the public orthodoxy is a secularism which becomes progressively more strident and demanding. Heathenism and gentilism are sitting on the same dais waiting to be officially introduced.

Two of Brownson's most important contributions to political theory reside in his speculations concerning constitutions, particularly the United States Constitution, and his conception of the United States as a territorial democracy. Earlier, under the influence of de Maistre, he supported the view that constitutions were generated, not made. In all nations the fundamental constitution is that of the people themselves. This is always the work of Providence using men and circumstance to express its will. He later veered away from this quasi-Hegelianism to mark in the United States the existence of two constitutions, the unwritten and the written, of which the former is the authentic constitution of the American people as a sovereign community. It is born with the nation, not made by it. The American nation exists as a historic fact prior to any written constitution. The unwritten constitution marked the genesis of the nation and already subsisted in the womb of English common law. The written constitution reflects the unwritten and, because of this, cannot be changed in its essentials without provoking the destruction of the nation.

Territorial democracy is a theory formulated in an extensive addendum to Brownson's critique of Locke, the state of nature, and the Social Contract. The distinguished members of the 1787 Convention, he suggested, had not realized that the French Revolution and its horrors were contained in the Social Contract; all modern red-republicanism, socialism, and communism were implicit in the French Revolution. They failed to recognize the poison contained in the phrase "sovereignty of the people" which was, in their sense, so innocent and just. This notion of sovereignty is derived from the social contract by which men in the state of nature establish society. But there is no contract since there is no state of nature. Society is the natural state of man. Men are nowhere found outside society and society nowhere found without government. Brownson insists society is a living organism, not a congeries of atoms. Authority does not emanate from the people. It emanates from God and is vested in the people, an organic people fixed to a given territory.

Mankind should not be equated with mere population but with nations fixed to the soil, to a given territory. The United States existed as a sovereign people, as a territorial people under English common law, distributed into distinct states.

The Union and the states were born together and can only exist together. Because of this Brownson maintains that, in the United States, the sovereign is neither the central government nor the states taken severally, but the United States in convention. This remarkable conception seeks to preserve the original spirit and structure of the American nation, though it is open to criticism for ignoring the necessary consequences of change, of which the Greek political thinkers were so painfully aware, and underemphasizing the fragility of actually existing political institutions.

The area in which Brownson allowed both his pedantry and inventiveness free reign was that of philosophy. There he often approached encyclopedic lunacy, but he gloried in theoretical argument, however much mischief it caused him. A good example is his theory of inspiration, which with the passage of time became the proverbial albatross around his neck. It is already found in *Charles Elwood*, where he explicitly states that God is known immediately through intuition. This proposition reflects the presence of Cousin as does his demonstration of God by means of the Ideas that is found in the same work. True to his Augustinian roots, Brownson repeats the admonition to "turn inwards" and there behold the light, the source of inspiration. Inspiration is defined as the spontaneous revelation of reason and is reflected in the universal beliefs of mankind and its ability to judge supernatural revelation. Though his notion of intuition was further refined in the wake of his encounter with the works of the Abbate Gioberti, it was still open to the charge of ontologism, a theory condemned by Rome.

Brownson labored to distance himself from Gioberti's formulation by indicating that there is no direct intuition of God but rather an intuition of Being (*Ens*) which is indirect, indefinite, and must be subjected to the work of reflection and demonstration before Being (*Ens*) can be identified with God. Though he endorsed Gioberti's formula "*Ens creat Existentias*" (Being creates Existences), Brownson again asserted that the identification of *Ens* and *Deus* is made through reflection and not intuition. In this way he attempted to preserve what was philosophically valuable in Gioberti's formulation without risking condemnation. Gioberti's ontologism and his violent assaults on the Jesuits served to compound the difficulty. Moreover, such a formulation would have great difficulty passing muster in any camp dominated by the influence of St. Thomas Aquinas.

Brownson was very much aware of the great influence and stimulating effect that the thought of Pierre Leroux exercised on him. His philosophical muse found its *métier* in the assimilation, modification, and extension of Leroux's pivotal doctrine of communion. Several later thinkers, perhaps even Voegelin, attempted variations on the theme. Still, Brownson remains in a special position as his analyses paved the way for later endeavors. He both extended Leroux's speculations and elaborated a novel corrective for his tilt toward pantheism—God's freedom—while suggesting that the Christian doctrine of purgatory anticipated Leroux's conception of history.

Man communes with other men and the world in three ways: with God through humanity, with men through his family and the State, and with nature through property. Man cannot live without an object, as life is jointly in *me* and the *not-me*, sparked by their inter-shock. To the disciples Jesus was the object, which is to say, the objective portion of their life by which their subjective life was developed. All men are then members of one another linked in solidarity. Brownson adds that solidarity is a temporal and a spatial phenomenon. It embraces all men in all ages and links the first and last man in indissoluble life.

Leroux's theory must be reversed. The human symbolizes the divine, not the divine the human. As man depends completely on the objective element that grounds him, his communion with God takes place not only on the natural but also on the supernatural plane. Brownson affirms that man is constituted as a rational existent due to the immediate presence of God, who is Creator, object, and light of his reason, providing him with the ability to know and to love. This follows Augustinian tradition, though it may seem to tilt toward ontologism, and resembles one of those medieval versions of the role and operations of the Agent Intellect, or an ectoplasmic residue of Emerson's Oversoul.

Brownson was a bold, if obsessive, thinker. In spite of his eccentricities and changes of course he made important contributions to several areas of human concern. No subject escaped the probings of his all-too-inquisitive mind. His speculations on god, man, sin, society and religion were, on the whole, penetrating, if not conclusive. His interpretations and variations on philosophies such as those of Cousin, Leroux, Gioberti, and others were acute and clarifying. The Cassandra-like warnings were often on target, predicting the depredations of radical democracy, statism, rampaging feminism, and ethnic division. Brownson foresaw the national fragmentation issuing from the melting-pot ideology as well as the advance of a noxious neo-paganism that excludes the supernatural. His interpretation of the United States as a territorial republic with substantial medieval roots and incursions into constitutional theory marked one of the high points of American political thought.

Though arguably not of a stature equal to Jonathan Edwards, C. S. Peirce, Santayana, or Royce as a theologian or philosopher,[4] and without the practical expertise of a John Adams or a Calhoun as a political thinker, Brownson remains a major American thinker, a man of astonishing versatility. His merit was to stop at all important ports-of-call; his legacy is a theoretical tapestry not lacking in profundity or verve. As a distinguished editor, writer, and combatant *pro ecclesia* he demonstrated that American Catholicism had come of age. His tragedy stems from a lack of wholeness, of completion: Brownson remained a prophet *manque*, a saint forming but never formed, a superb portrait left unfinished, an episodical philosopher of genius.

Epilogue

Ortega y Gasset, Isak Dinesen, and others have marked the ephemeral character of personality. We select one out of a multiplicity of possible faces and proceed to invent ourselves. Brownson selected faces according to circumstance. The reader has the impression of coming into contact with unfinished faces, sparks emitted by an elusive core. This is true of everyone to some extent. In Brownson it is an operational necessity. For all his bluntness, apparent lack of craft, and the simplicity of his rough-hewn exterior, one senses that it constitutes a facade, a protective shell—covering, who knows what—perhaps nothing.

Early in Brownson's career, Parke Godwin spoke of an unhappy lack of integrity of mind: "the great difficulty... with Mr. Brownson, is that he sees only one truth at a time or rather one side or aspect of truth, which he is driven to assert as the whole and only truth in the Universe.... [T]he absolute is his forte."[1] Brownson's notorious weathercock propensity may have been fostered by his lack of formal education and the mélange of Scripture and fantasy that took its place. His impressive fund of knowledge was an edifice built on a weak foundation. Perhaps this can in part explain the lack of theoretical continuity in his work; he takes a new acquisition that could be used to complete the edifice as the cornerstone of a new structure.

There is more continuity of theme than of philosophical substance in Brownson's thought. The theme is expanded to include the newly acquired view that, by its very addition, tends to modify the development and outcome of his argument. This is not to suggest that Brownson's thought is not undergirded by principle. But aside from the rules of logic, these principles are few and belong more to religion than to philosophy. They serve to establish the boundaries along which his speculation will develop.

Brownson formulated with celerity, often casting his thoughts into print without having fully digested the material involved, without having woven it into the fabric of his thought. Lowell, in A Fable for Critics, was able to express the idiosyncratic character of Brownson's mind: "He shifts quite about, then proceeds to expound that 'tis merely the Earth, not himself, that turns round."[2]

Everything becomes grist for his mills, which unlike God's, do not grind slowly, nor exceptionally fine, though they did produce an astonishing variety of products of wildly uneven quality.

The most important constants that characterized Brownson were his firm attachment to Church and Country. His conversion to Roman Catholicism was not reversed. His abiding passion was his thirst for salvation. The turn to crusty ultramontane conservatism was due more to his fear of Hell than to qualms concerning his status among Catholics. The outer darkness was more to be shunned than the world he abandoned on entering the Catholic fold. There were the examples of Lammenais, Lacordaire, and the Louvain ontologists who had been censured by Rome. Brownson's loyalty

to the Church perdured in spite of his controversies and disenchantment with individual Catholics.

He was attacked from many quarters, including the hierarchy and the Catholic press. When he entered the Church, he
found that in the United States it was headed, for the most
part, by cultural aliens with a marked distaste for American
customs, mores, and peculiarities. Educated Catholics looked
to England and France for intellectual and spiritual suste-
nance. Brownson thought poorly of both, skewering the genteel Newman and Veuillot, the rough ultramontane. While
early maintaining that a providential conjunction existed
between Catholicity and Americanism, he slowly veered away
from this position to hold that an intractable opposition separated them.

From early childhood, Brownson's interests, fantasies,
and ambitions involved religion. From his brief, disappoint-
ing encounter with Presbyterianism to his last discussion
with son Henry concerning the sin against the Holy Spirit, it
was the center around which he revolved. The youthful
episode in which he was overwhelmed by the weight of sin
and alienation may not have been completely overcome. His
works point in this direction. So do the utopian communities
he halfheartedly encouraged, possibly as a residue of his
early dream of bringing heaven down to earth, even at the
expense of property, marriage, and family. Much of his original enterprise of renewing and completing Christianity by
means of a new Christ, a new Church, and a new social
order became the point of departure for incursions into different areas of activity.

His distaste for industrialism and admiration for the
Southern ethos was not merely a product of his romanticism,
but a realization that the industrial, the technological, the
economic mind is alien to tradition. As Carl Schmitt has indi-

cated, it refuses to believe that prior to the reality of material things something transcendental—an authority from above—was already in existence. Privacy is destroyed. The excellent is dismissed: "everything will be enacted upon an open stage and before an audience of Papagenos."[3] Freedom, as Brownson indicates, vanishes into the maw of a voracious public orthodoxy that sets itself up as the ultimate authority.

Protestantism, in Brownson's opinion, was not a religion situated on the opposite pole of the spectrum from Catholicism; it was not a religion at all. To his mind it was the reaction of matter against spirit, State against Church, the world against its proper subjection to God. Yet his attacks skewer much which modernity considers laudatory. Protestantism is responsible for civil liberty, philosophy, industry, in effect, all earthly endeavors. It failed, Brownson suggests, when it moved toward unlimited freedom of thought, the deification of reason, and radical Pelagianism. The Pelagian separation of the natural from the supernatural, which he affirms has become nearly universal, promotes civil and religious license, prodding society in the direction of a noxious, egalitarian democracy.

While discarding Protestantism, at one point Brownson endeavored to concoct a religion of humanity following the lines endorsed by the French Revolution and its aftermath. Later, when he became convinced that reason did not suffice, that divine guidance and grace were necessary, the enterprise inspired him with repugnance. His chilling awareness of sin furthered his disenchantment and definitively separated him from his Transcendentalist past and its pastiche of bland humanism and oriental esoterica. His stress on God's freedom took him further. By denying necessity, the reduction of God to nature is rejected, as is the consequent conflation of the human and divine. As divine grace is absolutely necessary,

Jesus must be more than an ethereal symbol: He must exist and possess the attributes ascribed to him by orthodox Christianity. If this is so, then there must also exist an authoritative judge and interpreter of Christian belief. This is the Roman Catholic Church.

A convert at the age of forty-one, Brownson at first viewed his new faith as the vehicle to arrive at popular democracy. Later he saw it buttressing a constitution in danger of decomposition from materialism and democratic leveling. He accordingly attacked Come-Outerism as resting on flawed premises, ironically suggesting that if the Quaker doctrine of "the light within" were added to its ideology, it would be provided with a divine foundation. He later attacked the Free Religious Association as the successor to Come-Outerism, as radicals and universal agitators. Very much the intellectual and scholar, fascinated by abstruse speculation, he was nevertheless aware of the strong temptation to reduce Christianity to an impressive but all too human structure, and did not surrender to this seduction. As Christianity always is God-given, this enterprise would be tantamount to idolatry. Brownson's attacks on Newman and the Tractarians, for all their lack of theological subtlety, were primarily directed against what he perceived as their degradation of the Church to the status of a purely human institution.

Brownson did not agree with Father Hecker that reason and nature aspire to supernatural beatitude. They were, he felt, unable to do so without the added factor of grace. His episodical attacks on the Gallicanism of the American Church arose from his fear that the supernatural order was in danger of suffering an untimely eclipse. He may have foreseen the ugly utilitarian liturgies and social-center churches that presently afflict us. He never doubted that Catholicity affirmed the essential nature of religion nor did he question its authoritative status in religious matters. Though his love for the American Republic intermittently conflicted with his religious allegiance and must have caused no little inner turmoil, he continued to uphold the superiority of the spiritual realm over the material.

When he attacked the American Catholic press for their responsibility in lowering the tone of public discourse and propagating religious indifference, he spoke as an American Catholic. When he lauded honesty and plain dealing over the deviousness of some clergy, he was employing positive American traits to counter what he believed were foreign habits of mind. His role in the Know-Nothing controversy was guided by Christian principle as well as by his exalted conception of the American Republic. His enthusiastic advocacy of the Union during the Civil War was made within the boundaries of Catholic doctrine and natural law. Whatever exacerbations he might have been guilty of were compensated by his efforts in favor of the South in the aftermath of the conflict. Even his ambivalent defense of slavery as an existing institution guaranteed by the Constitution, scarcely admirable by today's standards, was offset by his moral condemnation of slavery buttressed by papal edicts.

When Christianity and democracy were identified or viewed as inseparable or allied, common areas of agreement were expeditiously discovered. The Church of the Future was a mixture of Church and State modeled somewhat eccentrically on the Society of Friends (Quakers). The temptation to conflate the political and religious remained strong and lasting. But when Brownson swerved in the opposite direction, he proposed that the Catholic Church remain neutral. It should not endorse democracy (or any political ideology), as this would transform it into a religious dogma and inject it into the bloodstream of the Christian faith. This admonition went unheeded. A contemporary writer can speak of "the transformation of the Roman Catholic Church from a bastion of the ancient regime into perhaps the world's foremost institutional defender of human rights."[4] Though well intentioned, this statement is surprisingly naive. The past two centuries have demonstrated that the rights of man are easily transformed into the right of the State to possess and control men.

Brownson came to reject egalitarian democracy for constitutional republicanism. When the great mass of the American people moved in the opposite direction, his view of the American people and Catholic Church began to change and his early hopes to fade. He was alive to the peril of humanitarian democracy, which dispenses with geographical boundaries, poses as Christian philanthropy, and identifies humanitarianism and Christianity. Only a small step to asserting that man is God! Very much alive to the danger presented by the ignoring of tradition, he protested against the efforts of "the present infidel movement" to abolish the Greek and Roman classics and transform education into a pure utilitarian and naturalistic endeavor, very similar to the lure of today's educational Emerald City. Kowlakowski has correctly marked those "powerful, cultural forces… pushing us towards unity, a barbarian unity built on the loss, the forgetting of tradition."[5] Brownson urged that the presence of the Catholic Church was necessary to the survival of the commonwealth that, as it rests on natural law, would wither in proportion to the decline of the Church's presence.

There undoubtedly is much of the novice and the *poseur* in Brownson. He thrived on exaggeration, bluster, and fanfaronade. Theodore Parker was not completely off the mark when he accused Brownson of being more a verbal index to Christianity than an authentic Christian. But even Parker admitted his intelligence, originality, and depth, asking Convers Francis whether he believed that Brownson was more original than Emerson as he had noticed that many of Emerson's ideas came from the *Boston Quarterly Review*.[6] His typically American traits—optimism, fascination with the new and bizarre, hyperactivity—came to be strangely blended with pessimism, a fascination with evil and the depredations of original sin. Whether a result of the many external pressures he had been subjected to or because of some inner fracture, Brownson believed he had been put in a corner, defending his right to be an American against Catholics and his right to be a Catholic against Americans.

He went from contending that the American character fitted Catholicity as key to lock, to the opposite pole affirming there was scarcely a trait in the American character, as practically developed, which was not hostile to Catholicity. But he did so as an American Catholic. In the late 1860's Brownson was still predicting that Christendom would eventually be established in the United States on a republican basis. To discourage intramural hostility, he decided in 1863 that the *Review* limit itself to questions of the day and avoid philosophy and theology. Nevertheless he took a strong position on religious liberty and, in July 1864, a short time prior to the promulgation of *Quanta Cura*, stated that all religions not *contra bonos mores* are equal before the state and entitled to full protection, a view adumbrating the Declaration on Religious Liberty of Vatican II. It was a measure that Brownson believed would strengthen, not weaken, the Church.

Though he was the advocate of several fleeting enthusiasms, Brownson usually set himself resolutely against the popular tide. He came to reject the harsh tenets of New England Calvinism as well as the ectoplasmic Christianity of Universalism. He vigorously defended the Irish immigrants while protecting American traditions and mores against the hostility of these same immigrants and their prelates. He opposed spiritism, the "New Age" fad of his day, at the height of its influence, marking its intimate connection with the other abominations of the epoch. At first sympathetic to feminism, Brownson later opposed it, considering it the latest port of call of the spirit of upset which ineluctably would move on to victimize the very structure of the family.

Within American Catholicism, Brownson set himself against the influence of French aristocracy when it presented a danger to the Church and probably the nation [Napoleon III's Mexican adventure held unsettling possibilities]. He also opposed the trend towards radical democracy when it threatened to lead to ochlocracy—a destination destructive to the nation's fabric, and constitutive of a pseudo-church alien to Catholic tradition. While defending Catholicity with vigor he did not hesitate to assail Catholic prelates, criticize John Henry Newman, and cavalierly dismiss Pope Pius IX's efforts to mediate between North and South.

Prior to the outbreak of hostilities Brownson attacked both abolitionists and Southern fire-eaters. After Fort Sumter he took a strong pro-Union stand and castigated Catholics for their lukewarm support of the Union cause—due, he believed, to the vested interests of the hierarchy and religious orders. After the Union victory, he energetically opposed Reconstruction as counterproductive, humiliating to the South, a means of cementing Northern industry in its privileged position, and a doorway to "Africanization" of the South. Both his theory of territorial democracy and of the written Constitution as arising from and dependent on the unwritten Constitution provided a barrier against wild interpretation, a perennial temptation.

Brownson was a man of his epoch and of ours, strangely irrelevant to the near-century straddling the two Vatican Councils. This fact, together with his erratic character, unexpected turns, and the explosive quality of many of his views, certainly contributed to the unmerited obscurity to which his person and thought have been consigned. He deserves to be rescued from the outer darkness for his many contributions to culture, religion, and the commonweal, and his status as the most stimulating and influential of American Catholic thinkers. But perhaps most of all, he should be reinstated because of his Socratic role as "gadfly"—a cantankerous sign of contradiction.

Bibliography

PRIMARY SOURCES

Maunscript Material: Microfilm of the Brownson Papers in the archives of the Notre Dame University Library were receledared and microfilmed under the sponsorship of the National Historical Publications Commission.

The Works of Orestes A. Brownson. Collected and arranged by Henry F. Brownson. Detroit: Thorndike Nourse, 1882-87. 20 Volumes.

Brownson, Henry F. *Orestes A. Brownson's Early Life (1803-1844)*. Detroit: H.F.Brownson, 1898.

_____. *Orestes A. Brownson's Middle Life (1845-1855)*. Detroit: H.F. Brownson, 1899.

_____. *Orestes A. Brownson's Latter Life (1855-1876)*. Detroit: H.F. Brownson, 1900.

Brownson, Orestes A. *Selected Essays*. Edited by Russell Kirk. Chicago: Henry Regnery Co., 1955.

_____. *Selected Writings*. Edited by Patrick Carey. New York: Paulist Press, 1991.

_____. *The Boston Quarterly Review (1838- 1842).*

_____. *Brownson's Quarterly Review (1844-1864, 1873-1875).*

SECONDARY SOURCES

Albanese, Catherine L. (Ed.). *The Spirituality of American Transcendentalists.* Macon: Mercer University Press, 1988.

Barbour, Brian M. (Ed.). *American Transcendentalism: An Anthology of Criticism.* South Bend: University of Notre Dame Press, 1973.

Boler, Paul F., Jr. *American Transcendentalism 1830-1860: An Intellectual Inquiry.* New York: G.P. Putnam's Sons, 1973.

Butler, Gregory S. *In Search of the American Spirit: The Political Thought of Orestes Brownson.* Carbondale: Southern Illinois University Press, 1992.

Conroy, Paul. *Orestes A. Brownson: American Political Philosopher.* Unpublished Ph.D. dissertation. St. Louis University, 1937.

Corrigan, Sister Felicia. *Some Social Principles of Orestes A. Brownson.* Washington: Catholic University Press, 1939.

Cross, Robert C. *The Emergence of Liberal Catholicism.* Cambridge: Harvard University Press, 1958.

Ellis, John Tracy. *American Catholicism.* New York, 1955.

Farrell, Bertin. *Orestes A. Brownson's Approach to the Problem of God.* Washington: Catholic University Press, 1950.

Frothingham, Octavius Brooks. *Transcendentalism in New England*. New York: G.P. Putnam's Son's, 1876. Reprint. New York: Harper Torchbooks, 1959.

Gilhooley, Leonard. *Contradiction and Dilemma: Brownson and the American Idea*. New York: Fordham University Press, 1972.

_____ (Ed.). *No Divided Allegiance: Essays in Brownson's Thought* New York: Fordham University Press, 1980.

Gohdes, Clarence E.F. *The Periodicals of American Transcendentalism*. Durham: Duke University Press, 1931.

Gower, Joseph F. and Leliaert, Richard M. (Eds.). *The Brownson-Hecker Correspondence*. South Bend: University of Notre Dame Press, 1979.

Hutchinson, William R. *The Transcendentalist Ministers*. New Haven: Yale University Press, 1959.

Kirk, Russell. *The Conservative Mind: From Burke to Santayana*. 6th Revised Edition. South Bend: Gateway, 1978.

Lapati, Americo D. *Orestes A. Brownson*. New York: Twayne, 1965.

Laski, Harold. *The American Democracy: A Commentary and an Interpretation*. New York: Viking, 1948.

Marshall, Hugh. *Orestes Brownson and the American Republic: An Historical Perspective*. Washington: Catholic University Press, 1971.

Maynard, Theodore. *Orestes Brownson: Yankee, Radical, Catholic*. New York: Macmillan, 1943.

McCarthy, James Leonard. *Rhetoric in the Works of Orestes Brownson*. Unpublished Ph.D dissertation. Fordham University, 1961.

McDonnell, James M. *Orestes A. Brownson and Nineteenth-Century Catholic Education*. New York: Garland, 1988.

Michel, Virgil. *The Critical Principles of Orestes Brownson*. Washington: Catholic University Press, 1918.

Miller, Perry. *The Transcendentalists: An Anthology*. Cambridge: Harvard University Press, 1950.

Raemers, Sidney A. *America's foremost Philosopher*. Unpublished Ph.D dissertation. St Anselm's Priory, Washington D.C.

Roemer, Lawrence. *Brownson and Democracy and the Trend Towards Socialism*. New York: Philosophical Library, 1953.

Ryan, Thomas R. *Orestes A. Brownson: A Definitive Biography*. Huntington, Ind.: Our Sunday Visitor, 1976.

————. *Orestes A. Brownson: The Pope's Champion in America*. Chicago: Franciscan Herald Press, 1990.

Sargent, Daniel. *Four Independents*. New York: Sheed and Ward, 1935.

Schlesinger, Arthur M., Jr. *Orestes A. Brownson: A Pilgrim's Progress*. Boston: Little, Brown, 1939.

Sennott, Thomas M. *They Fought the Good Fight: Orestes A. Brownson and Father Feeney*, 1988.

Sveino, Per. *Orestes A. Brownson's Road to Catholicism*. New York: Humanities Press, 1970.

Tyler, Alice F. *Freedom's Ferment*. Minneapolis: Bruce, 1944.

Whalen, Sister Rose Gertrude (Doran). *Some Aspects of the Influence of Orestes Brownson on His Contemporaries.* South Bend: University of Notre Dame Press, 1933.

Notes

PROLOGUE

1. Russell Kirk, *The Conservative Mind*, 6th Revised edition (South Bend: Gateway, 1978), p. 214.

2. *The Catholic World*, XLV (May 1887), p. 204.

3. Letter of Rev. Reuben Smith to the Editor of the *Princeton Review*, XXX (April 1858), p. 392.

4. *The Convert*. In *The Works of Orestes A. Brownson*, collected and arranged by Henry F. Brownson (Detroit: Thorndike House, 1884), Vol. 5, pp. 83-84.

5. *Brownson's Quarterly Review* (hereafter *BrQr*), July 1862. *Works* 14, pp. 577-89.

CHAPTER ONE

1. *The Convert*, p. 3.

2. *The Convert*, pp. 3-4. The most informative source is Thomas R. Ryan, *Orestes A. Brownson: A Definitive Biography* (Indianapolis: Our Sunday Visitor, 1976), pp. 16-17f.

3. *The Convert*, pp. 4-5. Arthur M. Schlesinger, Jr., *Orestes A. Brownson: A Pilgrim's Progress* (Boston: Little, Brown, 1939), pp. 4-6.

4. *The Catholic Historical Review*, XLIX (January 1964), p. 529

5. Ryan, pp. 23-24. *The Convert*, pp. 9-11.

6. *The Convert*, p.12.

7. Henry F. Brownson, *Orestes A. Brownson's Early Life* (Detroit: H.F. Brownson, 1898), pp. 18-19.

8. Schlesinger, pp. 11-12. Ryan, p. 35f.

9. *The Convert*, p. 19.

10. *The Convert*, pp. 25-26.

11. *The Convert*, p. 36.

12. *Early Life*, p. 31ff.

13. Per Sveino, *Orestes A. Brownson's Road to Catholicism* (New York: 1970), p. 43, n. 66.

14. "Dr. Brownson and the Workingman's Party Fifty Years Ago." *The Catholic World*, XLV (May 1887), p. 224. *Early Life*, pp. 373, 381.

15. Schlesinger, pp. 41, 153.

16. January 8, 1829. Ryan, p. 53.

17. *Early Life*, p. 41

18. *The Convert*, p. 56.

19. *The Convert*, pp. 39-40.

20. *The Convert*, p. 59.

21. *The Convert*, pp. 50-55.

22. *The Convert*, p.43.

23. *The Convert*, p. 42.

24. *The Convert*, pp. 60-62. Ryan, p. 57f.

25. Schlesinger, pp. 26-27.

26. "Lacordaire and Catholic Progress." *BrQR* (July 1862). *Works* 20, pp. 258, 262.

27. Theodore Maynard, *Orestes Brownson: Yankee, Radical, Catholic* (New York: Macmillan, 1943), pp. 47, 54.

28. *The Convert*, p. 48.

29. Ryan, pp. 70-712. Citing microfilm of *Brownson Papers*, roll 9.

30. *The Convert*, pp. 64-65.

31. *The Convert*, pp. 66, 68.

32. *The Convert*, p. 87.

33. *Early Life*, pp. 111-12, 114-15.

34. Maynard, p. 55.

35. Schlesinger, p. 36f.

Chapter Two

1. *Charles Elwood or The Infidel Corrected. Works* 4, p. 177, 196-97; "Charles Elwood Reviewed," *Boston Quarterly Review* (hereafter *BQR*) (April 1842). *Works* 4, p. 333.

2. *Charles Elwood*, p. 316.

3. *Charles Elwood*, p. 206.

4. Peirce's notion of *musement* was first presented in a paper written in 1908: "A Neglected Argument for the Reality of God," *Collected Papers of Charles Sanders Peirce*, edited by Charles Hartshorne and Paul Weiss (Cambridge: Harvard University Press, 1931-35), 6.465, 6.458, 6.488.

5. The Ideas "are out of the soul, out of the *me*, and not in it." "Charles Elwood Reviewed," pp. 336, 341.

6. *Charles Elwood*, pp. 266-67.

7. "Elwood Reviewed," pp. 347-48.

8. *Charles Elwood*, p. 277.

9. *Charles Elwood*, p. 224.

10. *Charles Elwood*, p. 293.

11. *Charles Elwood*, pp. 294-95.

12. *Charles Elwood*, pp. 296-98.

13. *BQR* I,1 (1838), p.125.

14. *Charles Elwood*, p. 291.

15. *Charles Elwood*, p. 303

16. *Charles Elwood*, p. 233.

17. *Charles Elwood*, p. 251.

18. *Charles Elwood*, p. 261.

19. *Charles Elwood*, pp. 282-83.

20. In the Lurianic tradition of Kabbalah an act of creation is possible only through "the entry of God into Himself," that is, through an act of *Tsimtsum*, whereby "He contracts Himself and so makes it possible for something which is not *Ein-Sof* (Infinite) to exist." Gershom Scholem, *Kabbalah* (New York: Quadrangle, 1974), p. 129ff.

21. *Charles Elwood*, p. 281.

22. "Elwood Reviewed," p. 317.

23. "Elwood Reviewed," p. 325.

24. "Elwood Reviewed," p. 325.

25. "Elwood Reviewed," p. 338.

26. "Synthetic Philosophy," *Works* 1, pp. 58-129.

27. "Elwood Reviewed," p. 357.

28. *New Views of Christianity, Society, and the Church. Works* 4, p. 2. "Review of New Views," *BQR* (January 1842). *Works* 4, p. 58.

29. "Review of New Views," p. 5.

30. "Review of New Views," p. 10.

31. "Reviews of New Views," pp. 13-14, 17.

32. "Review of New Views," p. 22.

33. "Review of New Views," p. 23.

34. "Review of New Views," pp. 24, 44.

35. "Review of New Views," p. 33.

36. "Review of New Views," p. 39.

37. "Review of New Views," p. 45.

38. "Review of New Views," p. 47.

39. "Review of New Views," p. 45.

40. C.S. Peirce, "How to Make Our Ideas Clear," *Collected Papers*, 5.389, 5.390, 5.402, 5.411, 5.412.

41. "Review of New Views," pp. 46-47.

42. "Review of New Views," pp. 57-58.

43. "Review of New Views," pp. 64-65.

44. "Review of New Views," pp. 71-72, 75.

45. "Review of New Views," pp. 77-78.

Chapter Three

1. Lewis Mumford, *The Golden Day* (New York: W.W. Norton, 1926), p. 87.

2. William R. Hutchinson, *The Transcendentalist Ministers* (New Haven: Yale University Press, 1958), p. 2.

3. Hutchinson, p. 5ff.

4. Hutchinson, pp. 9-12.

5. Cited by Frederick Ives Carpenter, "Transcendentalism." *American Transcendentalism: An Anthology of Criticism*, ed. by Brian M. Barbour (South Bend: U. of Notre Dame Press, 1973), p. 23.

6. Hutchinson, p. 28, n. 10.

7. Kirk, p. 210.

8. Octavius Brooks Frothingham, *Transcendentalism in New England: A History* (New York: G.P. Putnam's Sons, 1876). Reprint (New York: Harper Torchbooks, 1959) pp., 51-52, 87-96, 103-107.

9. "From Jonathan Edwards to Emerson." *New England Quarterly*, XIII (December 1940), pp. 589-617.

10. Hutchinson, pp. 47, 52, n. 1. Many traces of German thought can be found in several of the Transcendentalists. Refer to Rene Wellek, "The Minor Transcendentalists and German Philosophy," *Anthology*, pp. 104-119.

11. Hutchinson, p. 63.

12. *Christian Examiner*, XXI (September 1836), pp. 34-38. Georges J. Joyaux, "Victor Cousin and American Transcendentalism." *Anthology*, p. 129ff.

13. Joyaux, p. 129ff.

14. *The Spirituality of American Transcendentalists*, edited with introduction and notes by Catherine L. Albanese (Macon: Mercer University Press, 1988), pp. 7-8, 239f.

15. Cited by Ryan, p. 171.

16. Frothingham, p. 171.

17. Albanese, p. 16.

18. Mumford, pp. 89, 105.

19. Sveino, pp. 113-114.

20. Paul F. Boler, Jr., *American Transcendentalism, 1830-1860: An Intellectual Inquiry* (New York: G.P. Putnam's Sons, 1973), pp. 16, 19, 28-29ff. Charles R. Crowe, "The Unnatural Union of Phalansteries and Transcendentalists." Barbour, p. 149.

21. Albanese, p. 243.

22. Albanese, p. 256.

23. Albanese, pp. 271-73.

24. David Bowers, "Democratic Vistas." Barbour, p. 11.

25. "Democratic Vistas," pp. 11-12. Frederick Ives Carpenter, "Transcendentalism." Barbour, p. 31.

26. Cited by Carpenter, p. 31.

27. Cited by Carpenter, *Anthology*, p. 30.

28. *BQR* (January 1839), p. 106. Sveino, p. 168.

29. Cameron Thompson, "John Locke and New England Transcendentalism." Barbour, p. 84.

30. "John Locke and New England Transcendentalism." Barbour, p. 94.

31. Arthur M. Schlesinger, Jr., "Transcendentalism and Jacksonian Democracy." Barbour, p. 139.

32. "Transcendentalism and Jacksonian Democracy." Barbour, p. 141.

33. Henry James, "Emerson." Barbour, pp. 257-58, 272.

34. Boler, p. xiv.

35. Hutchinson, p. 81.

36. "The Dial," *BQR* (January 1841), pp. 131-132.

37. "Transcendentalism, or the Latest Form of Infidelity," *BrQr* (July 1845), p. 15. *Works*, 6, p. 42. "Transcendentalism Concluded," *BrQr* (July 1846), pp. 369, 428. *Works*, 6, pp. 102, 113, 127-128.

Chapter Four

1. Ralph Waldo Emerson, "Nature." *Ralph Waldo Emerson, Essays and Lectures*, edited by Joel Porte (New York: the Library of America; 1983), p. 10.

2. "Nature," pp. 28-29.

3. "Nature," p. 32.

4. "Nature," p. 34.

5. "Nature," pp. 37-38.

6. "Nature," pp. 41, 48.

7. Ralph Waldo Emerson, "The Divinity School Address." *Essays and Lectures*, p. 80.

8. "The Divinty School Address," p. 87.

9. "The Divinity School Address," pp. 88-89.

10. "The Divinity School Address," p. 92.

11. Ralph Waldo Emerson, "The Transcendentalist." *Essays and Lectures*, pp. 195-97.

12. "The Transcendentalist," p. 198.

13. "The Transcendentalist," pp. 202-06, 208.

14. Ralph Waldo Emerson, "The Over-Soul." *Essays and Lectures*, pp. 385-86.

15. "The Over-Soul," p. 387.

16. "The Over-Soul," p. 392.

17. "The Over-Soul," p. 400.

18. Ralph Waldo Emerson, "New England Reformers." *Essays and Lectures*, pp. 594-95.

19. "New England Reformers," p. 607.

20. "New England Reformers," p. 608.

21. "New England Reformers," p. 602.

22. "New England Reformers," p. 599. Emerson's remarks remind the contemporary reader of Jean Raspail's novel, *The Camp of the Saints*, trans. by Norman Shapiro (New York: Scribners, 1975)

23. Ralph Waldo Emerson, "Uses of Great Men." *Essays and Lectures*, pp. 615-16.

24. "Uses of Great Men," p. 631.

25. Ralph Waldo Emerson, "Plato; or, the Philosopher." *Essays and Lectures*, p. 634.

26. "Plato; or the Philosopher," pp. 639-40.

27. "Plato; or the Philosopher," p. 645.

28. "Plato; or the Philosopher," p. 652.

29. Ralph Waldo Emerson, "Swedenborg; or the Mystic." *Essays and Lectures*, p. 665.

30. "Swedenborg; or the Mystic," p. 666.

31. "Swedenborg; or the Mystic," pp. 682, 685-86.

32. "Swedenborg; or the Mystic," p. 676.

33. Ralph Waldo Emerson, "Shakespeare; or the Poet." *Essays and Lectures*, p. 726.

34. Kirk, pp. 212-13.

35. Ralph Waldo Emerson "Napoleon; or, the Man of the World." *Essays and Lectures*, pp. 727-28, 743-44. "Goethe; or the Writer." *Essays and Lectures*, pp. 758, 760-61.

36. Ralph Waldo Emerson, "English Traits." in *Essays and Lectures*, pp. 825, 830, 838, 888, 893, 903.

37. "English Traits," pp. 799, 828, 848, 888, 893, 903.

38. "English Traits," pp. 795, 833, 930.

39. Refer primarily to "Fate." *Essays and Lectures*, p. 950, *et al.*

40. "English Traits," p. 923.

41. "English Traits," p. 922.

42. "English Traits," pp. 886-888.

43. "English Traits," pp. 889; 880-890.

44. "English Traits," p. 849.

45. *Essays and Lectures*, p. 1134.

Chapter Five

1. Schlesinger, p. 56. Sister Mary Rose Gertrude Whelan, *Some Aspects of the Influence of Orestes Brownson on His Contemporaries* (South Bend: U. of Notre Dame Press; 1933), p. 33.

2. *The Convert*, pp. 99-100. Ryan, p. 102.

3. *Early Life*, p. 151. Henry Brownson, more conservative, remarked that his father "made one mistake. He began his operations with a particular class... the workingmen, the Trade Unionists," p. 146.

4. "The Church of the Future." *Works*, 4, p. 59.

5. Microfilm of the *Brownson Papers*. Cited by Ryan, p. 116.

6. Cited by Schlesinger, p. 67.

7. *BQR* IV (January 1841), pp. 35-36.

8. *Early Life*, p. 152.

9. *Early Life*, p. 206.

10. Harold Laski, *The American Democracy: A Commentary and an Interpretation* (New York: Viking, 1948), p. 664. Also refer to Leonard Gilhooly, *Contradiction and Dilemma: Orestes Brownson and the American Idea* (New York: Fordham U. Press, 1972).

11. "Democracy," *BQR*, I, 44 (January 1838).

12. Schlesinger, pp. 77-78.

13. *Early Life*, pp. 180-81.

14. Schlesinger, p. 82.

15. "Democracy and Reform," *BQR* II, 508 (October 1839). "The Laboring Classes," *BQR* III, 370 (July 1840). "Grund's America," *BQR* (April 1838), p. 163.

16. Cited by Schlesinger, p. 91.

17. *The Convert*, pp. 102-103.

18. Cited by Maynard, pp. 91-92.

19. *BQR* III, p. 517 (October 1840).

20. *The Convert*, p. 111.

21. *Early Life*, p. 265.

22. *The Convert*, p. 120.

23. "Our Future Policy," *BQR* (January 1841). *Works*, 15, p. 129. Ryan, p. 193f.

24. "Popular Government," *Democratic Review* XII (May 1843). *Works*, 15, pp. 293-94. *Early Life*, pp. 302-303.

25. Schlesinger, p. 128, note 12. Cousin stated that Brownson possessed "a talent of thought and style which developed consistently promises to America a philosopher of the first order." *Fragments Philosophiques* I, vi.

26. Microfilm of the *Brownson Papers*, roll 9. Cited by Ryan, p. 247f.

27. "Reform and Conservatism," *BQR* (January 1842), p. 61. *Works*, 4, p..80.

28. The tales are "Mesmeric Revelation" and "X-ing a Paragrab." *Edgar Allen Poe: Poetry and Tales*, edited by Patrick F. Quinn (New York: The Library of America, 1984), pp. 717-27; 917-23.

29. *Journals* VI, p. 297. Cited by Schlesinger, p. 63, note 4.

30. "Two Articles From the Princeton Review." *BQR* III (July 1840).

31. The description is Maynard's, pp. 89-90.

32. *The Convert*, p. 124.

33. *The Convert*, pp. 130-31.

34. *The Convert*, pp. 131-32.

35. "Zanoni." *BQR* (July, 1842), pp. 358-59.

36. *The Convert*, pp. 137-40.

37. Maynard, p. 127.

38. Cited by Schlesinger, p. 148.

39. Alice F. Tyler, *Freedom's Ferment* (Minneapolis, 1944), pp. 166-95. Americo D. Lopati, *Orestes A. Brownson* (New York: Twayne; 1965), pp. 20-21.

40. Ryan, pp. 230-32.

41. "Democracy and Liberty." *Democratic Review*, XII (April 1943). *Works*, 15, pp. 258-81; "The Present State of Society." *Democratic Review*, XIII (July 1843). *Works*, 4, pp. 423-460. Isaac Hecker's

elder brother, John, was prepared to fund a pro-Calhoun paper in New York and wished Brownson to accept the post of editor. *Early Life*, pp. 334-339.

42. Schlesinger, p. 173.

43. *The Convert*, pp. 155-56.

44. "Hildreth's Theory of Morals." *BrQr* I (July 1844). *Works*, 14, p. 248. "Church Unity and Social Ameliorati

45. The Convert, pp. 157-58.

46. The Convert, p. 164.

Chapter Six

1. "Leroux on Humanity," *BQR* (July 1842). *Works* 4, p. 100.

2. "Leroux on Humanity," p. 102

3. "Leroux on Humanity," p. 115.

4. "Leroux on Humanity," pp. 116-17.

5. "Leroux on Humanity," p. 121.

6. "Leroux on Humanity," p. 124.

7. "Leroux on Humanity," pp. 126-27.

8. "Leroux on Humanity," pp. 128-30.

9. "Leroux on Humanity," p. 136.

10. "Hildreth's Theory of Morals," *BrQR* (July 1844). *Works* 14, p. 236.

11. "Hildreth's Theory of Morals," pp. 238, 240.

12. "Hildreth's Theory of Morals," p. 250.

13. "Hildreth's Theory of Morals," p. 254.

14. "The Mediatorial Life of Jesus," *BQR* (June 1842). *Works* 14, p. 236.

15. "The Mediatorial Life," p. 147.

16. "The Mediatorial Life," p. 148.

17. "The Mediatorial Life," pp. 150, 166.

18. "The Mediatorial Life," p. 160.

19. "The Mediatorial Life," p. 161.

20. "The Mediatorial Life," p. 167.

21. "Catholicity Necessary to Sustain Popular Liberty," *BrQR* (October 1845). *Works* 10, p. 1.

22. "Catholicity Necessary," p. 2.

23. "Catholicity Necessary," pp. 12, 15.

24. "The Present State of Society," *Democratic Review* (July 1843). *Works*, 4, p. 424

25. "The Present State of Society," p. 426.

26. "The Present State of Society," p. 426.

27. "Come-Outerism: or the Radical Tendency of the Day," *BrQR* (July 1844). *Works* 14, p. 431f.

28. "Come-Outerism," p. 436.

29. "Come-Outerism," p. 452.

30. "Come-Outerism," p. 557.

31. "Newman's Theory of Christian Doctrine," *BrQR* (January 1847).*Works* 14, pp. 40, 44, 51, 73.

32. "Newman's Development of Christian Doctrine," *BrQR* (July 1846). *Works* 14, p. 16.

33. "Newman's Development," pp. 22-23.

34. "Newman's Development," p. 12.

35. "The Dublin Review on Development," *BrQR* (October 1847). *Works* 14, pp. 76, 81.

36. "The Dublin Review," p. 111.

37. Ottis Ivan Schreiber, "Appendix." *John Henry Cardinal Newman, An Essay on the Development of Christian Doctrine* (New York: Longmans, Green & Co., 1949), pp. 417-35.

38. "Constitutional Government," *BQR* (January 1842). *Works* 15, p. 231.

39. "Constitutional Government," p. 240.

40. "Constitutional Government," pp. 244, 257.

41. "Democracy and Liberty," *Democratic Review* (April 1843). *Works* 15, p. 274.

42. "Democracy and Liberty," p. 279.

43. "Democracy and Liberty," p. 280.

44. "Demogogism," *BrQR* (January 1844). *Works* 15, pp. 435f, 440.

45. "Demagogism," p. 444.

Chapter Seven

1. *The Brownson-Hecker Correspondence*. Edited with an introduction by Joseph F. Gower and Richard M. Leliaert (South Bend: U. of Notre Dame Press, 1979). Brownson to Hecker (June 6, 1844), p. 103.

2. Schlesinger, p. 193.

3. Hecker to Brownson (June 27, 1851). *Correspondence*, p. 153.

4. *The Convert*, pp. 186-89.

5. *Early Life*, p. 475f.

6. *Works* 14, p. 259; 28-34; 168, 175.

7. *Fortnightly Review* CXI (1922), p. 67. Cited by Ryan, p. 369.

8. *BrQR* V, I (1848), p. 51. *BrQR* VI, II (1849), p. 145. Gilhooley, pp. 135, 181.

9. Lopati, p. 120.

10. Schlesinger, pp. 208-09.

11. Maynard, p. 176.

12. "The Great Question," *BrQR* (October 1847). *BrQR* (January 1851) *et al.*

13. "Acton and Brownson: A Letter From America." *Catholic Historical Review* (January 1964), p. 530.

14. Schlesinger, pp. 209-10.

15. Whelan, p. 85.

16. Maynard, p. 154.

17. Cited by Gilhooley, p. 123.

18. *The Convert*, pp. 170-71.

19. *The Convert*, pp. 193-95.

20. "Cooper's Way of the Hour," *BrQR* (July 1851). *Works* 16, pp. 329-330.

21. *The Convert*, pp. 197-99.

22. "The Native Americans," *Works* 18, p. 26. Also 10, 20, 15, 574, *et al.*

23. Schlesinger, p. 215.

24. Ryan, p. 413.

25. "Questions of the Soul," *BrQR* (April 1855). *Works* 14, p. 538.

26. "Questions of the Soul," p. 547.

27. "Aspirations of Nature," *BrQR* (October 1857). *Works* 14, pp. 553-56; 559.

28. Gilhooley, p. 169.

29. Henry F. Brownson, *Orestes A. Brownson's Middle Life (1845-1855)* (Detroit: H. F. Brownson, 1899), pp. 471-73.

30. Cited by Ryan, p. 508.

31. Cited by Schlesinger, pp. 217-18.

32. Maynard, p. 169.

33. *Works* 1, pp. 423, 455, 447. *Works* 2, p. 493.

34. *Works* 2, pp. 38, 58, 439. Rev. Bertin Farrell, *Orestes Brownson's Approach to the Problem of God* (Washington: The Catholic University of America Press, 1950), pp. 56-58. "Brownson's demonstration consists in establishing a double identity: the identity of necessary ideas with necessary being, and the identity of necessary being with God" (p. 62).

35. Farrell, p. 64.

36. Maynard, p. 225.

37. Ryan, pp. 444-47.

38. *Middle Life*, pp. 548-50.

39. "Letter From America," p. 527.

40. Maynard, p. 210, note 2.

CHAPTER EIGHT

1. Refer to my *Donoso Cortes: Cassandra of the Age* (Grand Rapids: Eerdmans, 1995).

2. "Socialism and the Church," *BrQR* (January 1849). *Works* 10, p. 81.

3. "Socialism and the Church," p. 83.

4. "Willicroft, or Protestant Persecution," *BrQR* (January 1853). *Works* 10, p. 403. "Protestantism in Government," *BrQR* (April 1852). *Works* 10, pp. 428-30.

5. "Bishop Fenwick," *BrQR* (October 1846). *Works* 14, p. 473.

6. "Archbishop Spaulding," *BrQR* (January 1874). *Works* 14, p. 513.

7. "Socialism and the Church," pp. 82-83.

8. "Socialism and the Church," pp. 88-89. Citing *BrQR* (January 1840), pp. 117-19.

9. "Socialism and the Church," p. 93.

10. "Socialism and the Church," p. 106.

11. "Socialism and the Church," p. 110.

12. "Liberalism and Socialism," *BrQR* (April 1855). *Works* 10, p. 123.

13. "Liberalism and Socialism," p. 130.

14. "Liberalism and Socialism," p. 148.

15. "Liberalism and Socialism," p. 130.

16. "Liberalism and Socialism," p. 154.

17. "Liberalism and Socialism," p. 155.

18. "Liberalism and Socialism," p. 160.

19. "Rights and Duties," *BrQR* (October 1852). *Works* 14, pp. 293-94.

20. "Rights and Duties," p. 297.

21. "Rights and Duties," pp. 301, 310.

22. *The Spirit Rapper* (1854). *Works* 9, p. 14.

23. *The Spirit Rapper*, pp. 29-30.

24. *The Spirit Rapper*, p. 67.

25. *The Spirit Rapper*, pp. 57, 65.

26. *The Spirit Rapper*, p. 67.

27. *The Spirit Rapper*, pp. 100-01.

28. *The Spirit Rapper*, p. 139f.

29. "Spiritism and Spiritists," *Catholic World* (June 1869). *Works* 9, p. 350.

30. "Christianity and Heathenism," *BrQR* (January 1852). *Works* 10, pp. 361-62.

31. "Christianity and Heathenism," p. 363.

32. "Christianity and Heathenism," pp. 380, 364.

33. "Christianity and Heathenism," pp. 385-86.

34. "Christianity and Heathenism," p. 390.

35. "Protestants in the Sixteenth Century," *BrQR* (April 1856). *Works* 10, p. 524.

36. "Protestants in the Sixteenth Century," p. 525.

37. "Ventura's Funeral Oration," *BrQR* (April 1848). *Works* 10, p. 69.

38. "Ventura's Funeral Oration," pp. 72, 76.

39. "The Higher Law," *BrQR* (January 1851). *Works* 17, p. 2.

40. "The Higher Law," p. 3.

41. "The Higher Law," p. 3.

42. "The Higher Law," p. 6.

43. "The Fugitive-Slave Law," *BrQR* (July 1851). *Works* 17, p. 18.

44. Aquinas, St. Thomas, *Summa Theologica*, 1-2, Q96, a. 2; Q93, a.3 ad 3; Q98, a.1; 2-2, Q69, a.2 ad 1. *et al.*

45. "The Fugitive-Slave Law," p. 26.

46. "Native-Americanism," *BrQR* (January 1845). *Works* 10, p. 19.

47. "Native-Americanism," p. 22.

48. "Native-Americanism," p. 24.

49. "Native-Americanism," p. 20.

50. "The Native Americans," *BrQR* (July 1854). *Works* 18, pp. 282-83. "The Know-nothings," *BrQR* (1854-55). *Works* 18, pp. 301-09.

51. "The Native Americans," p. 286.

52. "The Know-Nothings," p. 354.

CHAPTER NINE

1. Henry F. Brownson, *Orestes A. Brownson's Later Life (1855-1876)* (Detroit: H. F. Brownson, 1900), pp. 31, 33.

2. Schlesinger, p. 221. "Separation of Church and State," *BrQR* Third N.Y. Series II (January 18, 1860). Works 12, p.409.

3. Schlesinger, p. 222.

4. *Later Life*, pp. 59-60. "Thebaud's Irish Rose," *BrQR* (October 1873). *Works* 18, p. 563.

5. Maynard, pp. 248-55. "The Mission of America," *Works* 11, p. 517. "Archbishop Hughes on the Catholic Press," *Works* 20, pp. 50-73.

6. Whelan, pp. 87-88.

7. Whelan, pp. 87-88. Ryan, p. 555.

8. Maynard, p. 277, note 31. *Works* 20, pp. 363-63; 309-10.

9. "Archbishop Hughes and the Catholic Press," *Works* 20, p. 54.

10. Microfilm of *Brownson Papers*, roll 9. Ryan, pp. 593-94; p. 823, note 21.

11. Maynard, p. 256.

12. *Works* 14, pp. 565, 570.

13. "Lacordaire and Catholic Progress," *BrQR* Third N.Y. Series, III (July 1862). *Works* 20, p. 253.

14. "The Giobertian Philosophy," *BrQR* National Series I (1864). *Works* 2, p. 221; *Works* 1, p. 404. In a period of roughly twelve years, Brownson wrote five articles on Gioberti's thought, a total of some 150 pages. Gioberti's philosophy *"porta un nome preciso: ontologismo"* as

Pignoloni states in his introduction to *Riforma Cattolica e Liberta* (Milano: Marzorati, 1969). Gioberti's polemic with the Jesuits occupied him for nearly three years (1846-48), from his *Prolegomeni*, five volumes of *Il Gesuita Moderno* (1846-47), and his *Apologia del Libro Intitulato il Gesuita Moderno* (1848).

15. *Latter Life*, p. 304. Ryan, p. 604f.

16. "Primitive Elements of Thought," *BrQR* (January 1859). *Works* 1, p. 418.

17. "Primitive Elements of Thought," p. 421. Brownson lectured at Seton Hall College in South Orange, New Jersey, where he belonged to its Board of Trustees from the granting of its charter (1861) to the year of his death. In the 1872-73 catalogue he is listed as Lecturer on Civil Polity. His actual lecturing career at the College was short-lived as the connections between Elizabeth and South Orange were inconvenient and the cost of a residence near the College was prohibitive. The lectures were discontinued. Yet his influence perdured. We find *Brownson's American Republic* used as the text for the Civil Polity course in the 1884-85 catalogue. *Latter Life*, pp. 548-49. Seton Hall University Archives.

18. "Various Objections Answered," *BrQR* (October 1861). *Works* 20, p. 137.

19. "The Existence of God," *BrQR* (April 1852). *Works* 1, p. 274. Ryan, p. 666f.

20. *Latter Life*, p. 525.

21. *Works* 12, pp. 220-21.

22. Ryan, p. 516. "Liberalism and Socialism," *BrQR* (April 1855). "Rome and the Peace," *BrQR* (July 1855).

23. Maynard, pp. 282-83.

24. Maynard, p. 284.

25. Sveino, p. 312.

26. W. Birbeck Wood, "American Civil War," *Encyclopedia Britannica* 14th ed., 1929. Vol 1, pp. 723-67; esp. 753-55.

27. *Works* 17, pp. 55-57.

28. Schlesinger, p. 247.

29. *Works* 17, p. 257.

30. "Slavery and the War," *BrQR* (October 1861). *Works* 17, p. 169. "Archbishop Hughes on Slavery," *BrQR* (January 1862). *Works* 17, p. 186.

31. Maynard, p. 319.

32. *Later Life*, p. 378.

33. *Later Life*, p. 367.

35. *Later Life*, pp. 367-68.

36. Maynard, p. 293f.

37. Ryan, pp. 190, 609, 639, *et al.*

38. *Later Life*, pp. 278, 432.

39. For a perceptive criticism of Lincoln and his administration see M.E. Bradford, "The Lincoln Legacy: A Long View," *Modern Age* (Fall 1980), pp. 355-363. Bradford especially censures "his distinction of style, to his habit of wrapping up his policy in the idiom of Holy Scripture, concealing within the Trojan Horse of his gasconade and moral superiority an agenda that would never have been approved if presented in any other form" (p. 362).

40. Maynard, p. 330.

41. Schlesinger, p. 253.

42. *Later Life*, p. 377.

43. *Works* 20, p. 215.

44. Microfilm of *Brownson Papers*, roll 9. Ryan, p. 823, note 28.

45. "Catholicity, Liberalism, and Socialism," *BrQR* (October 1862). *Works* 20, p. 280.

CHAPTER TEN

1. "Liberalism and Progress," *BrQR* (October 1864). *Works* 20, p. 346.

2. "Liberalism and Progress," p. 351.

3. "Liberalism and Progress," p. 352.

4. "Liberalism and Progress," p. 355.

5. "Liberalism and Progress," p. 360.

6. "The Church and Modern Civilization," *BrQR* (October 1856). *Works* 12, p. 135.

7. "La Mennais and Gregory XVI," *BrQR* (July 1859). *Works* 12, p. 218.

8. "La Mennais and Gregory XVI," pp. 220-21.

9. "Christianity or Gentilism," *BrQR* (January 1860). *Works* 12, pp. 286, 289.

10. "Brownson on the Church and the Republic," *BrQR* (January 1857). *Works* 12, p. 37.

11. "Brownson on the Church and the Republic," pp. 53, 57-58.

12. "Christian Politics," *BrQR* (April 1860). *Works* 12, p. 326.

13. "Christian Politics," p. 327.

14. "Christian Politics," p. 345.

15. "Rights of the Temporal," *BrQR* (October 1860). *Works* 12, pp. 401-02, 405.

16. "Slavery and the Incoming Administration," *BrQR* (January 1857). *Works* 17, p. 56.

17. "The Slavery Question Once More," *BrQR* (April 1857). *Works* 17, p. 92.

18. "Slavery and the War," *BrQR* (October 1861). *Works* 17, pp. 156-57.

19. "Slavery and the War," p. 164.

20. "Catholics and the Anti-Draft Riots," *BrQR* (October 1863). *Works* 17, p. 446.

21. "The President's Message and Proclamation," *BrQR* (January 1864). *Works* 17, pp. 522, 533.

22. *Abraham Lincoln: Speeches and Writings 1859-1865* (New York: The Library of America, 1989), p. 358.

23. *Abraham Lincoln*, pp. 291-92, 316, 341.

24. *Abraham Lincoln*, p. 353ff.

25. *Abraham Lincoln*, pp. 368, 395.

26. *Abraham Lincoln*, p. 571.

27. "Emancipation and Civilization," *BrQR* (April 1862). *Works* 17, p. 259.

28. "Emancipation and Civilization," p. 260.

29. "Emancipation and Civilization," p. 267.

30. "Slavery and the Church," *BrQR* (October 1862). *Works* 17, p. 330.

31. "Slavery and the Church," p. 352.

32. "Archbishop Hughes on Slavery," p. 208.

33. "Catholics and the Anti-Draft Riots," pp. 414-15.

34. "Catholics and the Anti-Draft Riots," p. 436.

35. "Catholics and the Anti-Draft Riots," pp. 437-38.

36. "Catholics and the Anti-Draft Riots," p. 443.

37. "Catholics and the Anti-Draft Riots," p. 444.

38. "The Federal Constitution," *BrQR* (January 1864). *Works* 17, pp. 480, 488.

39. "The Federal Constitution," p. 497.

40. "The Federal Constitution," p. 501.

41. "Political Constitutions," *BrQR* (October 1847). *Works* 15, pp. 562-63.

CHAPTER ELEVEN

1. Maynard, p. 336. *Later Life*, p. 490.

2. Schlesinger, p. 256.

3. Ryan, p. 637.

4. Fr. John Courtney Murray, *We Hold These Truths* (New York: Sheed and Ward, 1960).

5. "Civil and Religious Freedom," *BrQR* (July 1864). *Works* 20, p. 313.

6. Maynard, p. 352, note 102.

7. Sir Robert Filmer, *Patriarcha and Other Political Works*. Edited by Peter Laslett (Oxford: Basil Blackwell, 1949), p. 42.

8. Refer to M.E. Bradford, "A Neglected Classic: Filmer's Patriarcha," in *Saints, Sovereigns, and Scholars*, edited by Herrera, Lehrberger and Bradford (New York: Peter Lang, 1993), pp. 273-78.

9. *Works* 18, pp. 30-33.

10. *Works* 15, p. 5. Roemer, pp. 36-37.

11. *Works* 18, pp. 185-86. Roemer, p. 59ff.

12. *The American Republic. Works*, 18, pp. 139-40.

13. Schlesinger, p. 266. *Works* 8, p. 279.

14. Microfilm of the *Brownson Papers*, roll 9. Ryan, p. 646.

15. "Abolition and Negro Equality," *BrQR* (April 1864). *Works* 17, pp. 537-560.

16. "Home Politics." *Works* 18, p. 597.

17. Schlesinger, p. 269.

18. *Latter Life*, pp. 606-07.

19. *Early Life*, pp. 220-22.

20. *Early Life*, p. 226.

21. "Religious Novels," and "Women vs. Women," *BrQR* (January 1873). *Works* 19, p. 508. "Religious Novels," *BrQR* (January 1873). *Works* 19, p. 567.

22. Maynard, p. 368.

23. *Fundamental Philosophy* (New York/Boston: D & J Sadlier & Co., 1858). *The Life of Christopher Columbus* (Detroit: H. F. Brownson, 1890).

24. Schlesinger, p. 273.

25. Brownson to Hecker, June 9, 1869. *Brownson-Hecker Correspondence*. Number 130, p. 269.

26. *Latter Life*, p. 448.

27. Maynard, p. 367.

28. Maynard, p. 398.

29. *Latter Life*, pp. 613-14.

CHAPTER TWELVE

1. *The American Republic* (1865). *Works* 18, pp. 3, 8.

2. *The American Republic*, p. 15.

3. *The American Republic*, pp. 39-40, 43.

4. *The American Republic*, p. 62.

5. *The American Republic*, p. 67.

6. *The American Republic*, p. 72.

7. *The American Republic*, pp. 74, 81f.

8. *The American Republic*, p. 113.

9. *The American Republic*, pp. 109-111.

10. *The American Republic*, p. 114.

11. *The American Republic*, pp. 131, 165.

12. *The American Republic*, pp. 140, 199.

13. *The American Republic*, pp. 170, 179, 190.

14. *The American Republic*, p. 185.

15. *The American Republic*, p. 211.

16. *The American Republic*, pp. 217. 211-15.

17. *The American Republic*, p. 222.

18. "The Democratic Principle," *BrQR* (April 1873). *Works* 18, p. 251.

19. "Count de Montalembert," *BrQR* (July 1874). *Works* 14, p. 521.

20. "Count de Montalembert," pp. 528-29.

21. "Count de Montalembert," p. 531.

22. "Count de Montalembert," p. 534.

23. "The Recent Events in France," pp. 498-99.

24. "Abolition and Negro Equality," p. 547.

25. "Abolition and Negro Equality," p. 551.

26. "Abolition and Negro Equality," p. 554.

27. "Abolition and Negro Equality," p. 559.

28. "Primeval Man," *Catholic World* (September 1869). *Works* 9, pp. 320-21.

29. "La Mennais and Gregory XVI," *BrQR* (July 1859). *Works* 12, p. 218.

30. "Primeval Man," p. 327.

31. "The Primeval Man Not a Savage," *BrQR* (April 1873). *Works* 9, p. 472.

32. "The Primeval Man Not a Savage," pp. 474-75.

33. "Darwin's Descent of Man," *BrQR* (July 1873). *Works* 9, p. 495. "True and False Science," *BrQR* (July 1873). *Works* 9, p. 517.

34. "The Woman Question" (Article I), *Catholic World* (May 1869). *Works* 18, pp. 381-83.

35. "The Woman Question," pp. 387-88.

36. "The Woman Question," p. 391.

37. "The Woman Question," p. 403.

38. "The Woman Question," p. 409.

39. "The Political State of the Country," *BrQR* (January 1873). *Works* 18, pp. 520-21, 523.

40. "The Political State of the Country," p. 523. "Constitutional Guarantees," *BrQR* (April 1874). *Works* 18, p. 57f. Brownson believed the Fourteenth Amendment contained a hidden agenda to extend the guarantees of the Fifth Amendment to the several states, allowing the federal government to restrain state regulation of trade and industry. Such was the case from 1884 on. The Fifteenth would destroy the state as a body politic. Both tend to merge the state in the Union and by doing so, convert the republic from a federal into a centralized republic or a pure democracy. Refer to Russell Kirk's *The Conservative Constitution* (Washington: Regnery, 1990), Chapter 12, pp. 174-88; *esp.* p. 179-81.

41. "At Home and Abroad," *BrQR* (October 1873). *Works* 18, p. 537.

42. "At Home and Abroad," p. 544.

43. "The Political Outlook," *BrQR* (January 1874). *Works* 18, p. 559.

44. "Madness of Anti-Christians," *BrQR* (January 1847). *Works* 14, pp. 417-18. "Unity and Philanthropy," *Catholic World* (January 1867). *Works* 14, p. 440.

45. "The Church as Organism," *BrQR* (January 1858). *Works* 12, p. 91.

46. "Political Outlook," p. 555.

47. "The Outlook at Home and Abroad," *BrQR* (October 1874). *Works* 18, pp. 568-69.

Chapter Thirteen

1. Walter Elliot, *The Life of Father Hecker* (New York: The Columbia Press, 1891). Vincent Heller, *The Yankee Paul: Isaac Thomas Hecker* (Milwaukee: Bruce, 1958). Joseph McSorley, *Isaac Hecker and His Friends* (New York: Paulist Press, 1972).

2. *The Browning-Hecker Correspondence*, edited with introduction by Joseph F. Gower and Richard M. Leliaert (South Bend: U. of Notre Dame Press, 1979), p. 20.

3. *Brownson-Hecker Correspondence*, p. 26.

4. *Brownson-Hecker Correspondence*, p. 36.

5. *Brownson-Hecker Correspondence*, pp. 45-46.

6. *The Brownson-Hecker Correspondence*, Hecker to Brownson (November 14, 1841), #1, p. 59.

7. Hecker to Brownson (December 19, 1942), #3, p. 62.

8. Hecker to Brownson (September 6, 1943), #7, pp. 68-69, n. 7.

9. Brownson to Hecker (September 2, 1843), #6, p. 66. Brownson to Hecker (September 11, 1843), #8, p. 69.

10. Hecker to Brownson (October 16, 1843), #12, p. 74. Brownson to Hecker (November 8, 1843), #13, p. 76.

11. Hecker to Brownson (December 14, 1843), #14, p. 78.

12. Brownson to Hecker (March 3, 1844), #17, p. 84. Hecker to Brownson (March 15, 1844), #18, p. 86.

13. Hecker to Brownson (May 16, 1844), #23, pp. 97-98.

14. Hecker to Brownson (October 1, 1845), #45, pp. 139-40.

15. Brownson to Hecker (June 6, 1844), #25, pp. 102-03. Hecker to Brownson (undated, ed. July 31, 1845), #42, p. 134.

16. Hecker to Brownson (August 24, 1844), #31, p. 115-16. Hecker to Brownson (August 17, 1844), #29, p. 111.

17. Hecker to Brownson (January 14, 1845), #34, p. 121. Hecker to Brownson (May 8, 1845), #36, p. 124. Hecker To Brownson (July 24, 1845), #39, p. 129.

18. Hecker to Brownson (July 29, 1851), #51, p. 155. Hecker to Brownson (September 14, 1854) #63, p. 167.

19. Brownson to Hecker (undated, ed. December 31, 1845), #42, p. 134.

20. Hecker to Brownson (April 16, 1855), #71, p. 180.

21. Brownson to Hecker (August 5, 1857), #80, pp. 194-95.

22. Hecker to Brownson (September 1, 1857), #81, p. 197.

23. Brownson to Hecker (September 29, 1857), #82, pp. 199-201.

24. Hecker to Brownson (October 24, 1857), #83, draft, p. 207.

25. Brownson to Hecker (July 1, 1871), #155, p. 306.

26. Brownson to Hecker (January 24, 1868), #102, pp. 233-35.

27. Brownson to Hecker (July 26, 1869), #134, p. 273.

28. Brownson to Hecker (undated, ed. February 4, 1868), #105, p. 240.

29. Brownson to Hecker (January 28, 1868), #103, pp. 237-38.

30. Brownson to Hecker (March 10, 1868), #107, pp. 242-43.

31. "The Catholic Doctrine of Justification." *Catholic World* VI (January 1868), pp. 433-41.

32. Brownson to Hecker (March 17, 1868), #109, pp. 245-46.

33. Brownson to Hecker (March 30, 1868), #113, p. 250.

34. *Brownson-Hecker Correspondence*, p. 256, n. 5.

35. Hecker to Brownson (January 30, 1870), #139, pp. 278-82.

36. Hecker to Brownson (January 30, 1870) #139, pp. 278-82.

37. Hecker to Brownson (January 30, 1870), draft, p. 285.

38. Brownson to Hecker (August 25, 1870), #142, pp. 291-92.

39. Brownson to Hecker (January 10, 1872), #170, pp. 323-24. Hacker to Brownson (January 30, 1872), #173, p. 326.

40. Brownson to Hecker (January 31, 1872), #174, pp. 328-29.

41. *Catholic World* XLV (July 1887).

CHAPTER FOURTEEN

1. Cited in Schlesinger, p. 63. n. 4.

2. Fr. John Courtney Murray, *We Hold These Truths: Catholic Reflections on the American Proposition* (New York: Sheed and Ward, 1960).

3. *We Hold These Truths.* Note especially pp. 79-96, 97-123, and 295-336. Fr. Murray asks the question: "how open can it (American society) afford to be and still remain a society; how many barbarians can it tolerate and still remain civil; how many 'idiots' can it include (in the classical Greek sense of the 'private person' who does not share in the public thought of the City), and still have a public life; how many idioms, alien to one another, can it admit, and still allow the possibility of civil conversation?" (p. 117).

4. Yet, it is surprising that Professor John E. Smith, who restricts "Classical American Philosophy" to Peirce, James, Royce and Dewey, fails to mention Brownson when addressing problems such as "rationality in religion," "the concept of religious experience," etc. "Experience, God and Classical American Philosophy." *American Journal of Theology and Philosophy*, vol. 14, no. 2 (May 1993), pp. 119-45.

EPILOGUE

1. *The Harbinger*, VI, 84 (January 15, 1848).

2. Cited by Clarence L. F. Gohdes, *The Periodicals of American Transcendentalism*, p. 42.

3. Carl Schmitt, *The Necessity of Politics*, Introduction by Christopher Dawson, translated by E.M. Codd (London: Sheed and Ward, 1931). p. 83.

4. George Weigel, "Catholicism and Democracy." *The Washington Quarterly* (Autumn 1985), p. 5.

5. Lezlek Kowlakowski, "Looking for the Barbarians." *Modernity on Endless Trial* (Chicago: University of Chicago Press, 1990), p. 25.

6. Gohdes, p. 183.

Index

1843 →

acumen p. 96.